UNIVERSITY OF NORTH CAROLINA
STUDIES IN COMPARATIVE LITERATURE

NUMBER 48

UNIVERSITY OF NORTH CAROLINA
STUDIES IN COMPARATIVE LITERATURE

Founded by Werner P. Friederich

For other volumes in this series see page 156

HERDER AND THE BEGINNINGS OF COMPARATIVE LITERATURE

BY

ROBERT S. MAYO

CHAPEL HILL
THE UNIVERSITY OF NORTH CAROLINA PRESS
1969

Printed in the Netherlands by Royal VanGorcum Ltd., Assen

ACKNOWLEDGMENTS

In the development of this book many persons have provided assistance and encouragement. Among these I wish to mention with gratitude Professors George C. Buck, Eugene H. Falk, Werner P. Friederich, Alexander Gillies, Henry H. H. Remak, and most especially Frank G. Ryder. I have also received personal financial assistance from Indiana University and the publication of this study has been aided by a grant from the University Research Council of the University of North Carolina.

TABLE OF CONTENTS

CHAPTER I

INTRODUCTION

The need for an historical study of their discipline has been felt by many comparatists for a long time. Professor René Wellek stressed this point in a recent article about comparative literature and went on to provide one of the best outlines of the subject now available.[1] Of the few handbooks which serve as an introduction to the field two devote a brief chapter to an historical survey.[2] For the rest one must rely upon various articles, whose authors by no means agree upon the starting point of modern comparative literature.

This is not altogether surprising. There has been considerable disagreement over the years about the meaning of the term 'comparative literature'; indeed, one of the few points of unanimity concerns the insufficiency or incorrectness of the term itself. Albert Guérard protests: "My attachment to the *principle* of Comparative Literature gives me the right to express my opinion that the *term* Comparative Literature is useless, dangerous, and ought to be abolished."[3] A few years earlier, however, he had declared: "So we must register our protest against the term Comparative Literature; and we must confess in the same breath that we have no better one to suggest."[4]

---

[1] René Wellek, "Begriff und Idee der Vergleichenden Literaturwissenschaft," *Arcadia* II (1967), pp. 229-247.
[2] Paul Van Tieghem, *La Littérature Comparée* (Paris, 1931), pp. 19-32. Claude Pichois et André-M. Rousseau, *La Littérature Comparée* (Paris, 1967), pp. 11-25.
[3] Albert L. Guérard, "Comparative Literature?," *Yearbook of Comparative and General Literature VII* (1958), p. 1.
[4] Albert L. Guérard, *Preface to World Literature* (New York, 1940), p. 14.

To this day no one has produced a satisfactory and practical alternative term, and few serious efforts are made to do so. The term already in use appears to have become too well established to be ousted. The best suggestion, one which has been made in several quarters, is simply the dropping of the word comparative as redundant. This is already the generally accepted practice for the critics who write for the weekly magazines and serious newspapers, but one cannot really expect the academic world to follow suit. Nevertheless some recent definitions of their field by comparatists tend to broaden the scope and make the boundary lines separating comparative literature from world literature and general literature almost invisible. Professor Wellek writes: "But I doubt that the attempt to distinguish between 'comparative' and 'general' literature, made by Van Tieghem, can succeed," and "Comparative Literature has become an established term for study of literature transcending the limits of one national literature."[1] Henry Remak concurs with this definition, but extends it further:

> Comparative literature is the study of literature beyond the confines of one particular country, and the study of the relationships between literature on the one hand and other areas of knowledge and belief, such as the arts (e.g., painting, sculpture, architecture, music, philosophy, history, the social sciences (e.g., politics, economics, sociology), the sciences, religion etc., on the other.[2]

For him the differences between comparative literature and world literature are of degree in space, time, quality and intensity, and of method, insofar as world literature, like general literature, prescribes no method. Apparently comparative literature may concern itself with representative modern authors, or with second-rate and minor authors, whilst world literature must adhere to the "great books".

This method for separating the two categories of literature is not altogether satisfactory, and Prof. Remak seems to be aware of this fact when he admits that: "Much of what we have been and shall be doing is,

[1] René Wellek, "The Crisis of Comparative Literature" *Comparative Literature. Proceedings of the second congress of the International Comparative Literature Association*, I, 150.
[2] Henry H. H. Remak, "Comparative Literature, Its Definition and Function," *Comparative Literature: Method and Perspective*, ed. N. Stallknecht and H. Frenz (Carbondale, 1961), p. 3.

in effect, comparative world-literature."[1] In emphasizing the fundamental difference of method between comparative literature and world literature he appears to have implicitly accepted a basic and quite simple fact, which many scholars in the field have overlooked. Comparative literature must always be secondary literature, whereas world literature is primary, original literature. Certainly Goethe took this view when he first coined the term 'Weltliteratur' in 1827.[2] Since that time no one appears to have seriously disputed the basic assumption that only original works of literature are eligible to be included in the ranks of world literature.

These characterizations of comparative and of world literature are, however, by no means universally accepted. As Prof. Remak points out, there is a fundamental disagreement between what he calls, for the sake of convenience, the French school and the American school of comparatists. Generally the former are far more restrictive in their use of the term. In an article in the first number of the "Revue de littérature comparée" Fernand Baldensperger laid out two specific lines of development for comparative literature – the tracing of themes through folklore and literature, and the tracing of the interrelations of certain works and movements.

A more recent statement from this school, and an equally authoritative one, stands in Jean-Marie Carré's foreword to M.-F. Guyard's handbook on comparative literature. "La littérature comparée n'est pas la comparaison littéraire." He then explains: "...elle est l'étude des relations spirituelles internationales, des *rapports de fait* qui ont existé entre Byron et Pouchkine, Goethe et Carlyle, Walter Scott et Vigny, entre les œuvres, les inspirations, voire les vies d'écrivains appartenant à plusieurs littératures."[3] And Prof. Guyard himself categorically states: "On le voit: littérature comparée n'est pas comparaison." Certainly it is unjust to suggest that all French comparatists take this somewhat limited view of comparative literature; some of the French contributions to the

[1] *Ibid.*, p. 12.
[2] Woldemar von Biedermann, ed., *Goethes Gespräche* (Leipzig, 1890), p. 46. cf. Fritz Strich, Goethe und die Weltliteratur (Bern, 1946), p. 16.
[3] M.-F. Guyard, *La Littérature comparée* (Paris, 1951), p. 5.

3

Proceedings of the ivth Congress of the International Comparative Literature Association and the work of René Étiemble demonstrate clearly that Frenchmen can be as broadminded as comparatists from any other nation. The wider view of comparative literature will suit the purposes of this study better than the more restricted approach.

The disagreement about the term world literature goes somewhat deeper and was first crystallized about forty years ago by Ernst Merian-Genast.[1] He was able to distinguish three different accepted meanings for the term. The first type, which he labelled as the cosmopolitan, refers to that Goethean, supra-national literature such as appeared in Roman times or in the Christian middle ages. Implied in this view is the abolition of all national flavour, and conformity to general rules. The second type, to which he attaches the description canonical, refers to those works which have an effect beyond both their time and their place of origin. The assumption underlying this version is that "das Schöne" is something absolute and relies upon what Boileau describes as the "consentement universel". The third type is nothing less than: "die Gesamtheit des dichterischen Schaffens der Menschheit überhaupt." The completeness of this third view stems "aus der Überzeugung, dass jedes Kunstwerk als solches seinen Wert in sich trägt und nicht gleichsam erst von aussen die Übereinstimmung mit einem ein für allemal fixierten Schönheitsideal empfängt."[2] In support of this interpretation he quotes the Goethean Xenion:

> Gleich sei keiner dem andern, doch gleich sei jeder dem Höchsten:
> Wie das zu machen? Es sei jeder vollendet in sich.

Artistic merit is to be judged by the intensity of expression and such an organic concept of world literature allows for differences of taste in both the author and the reader. Merian-Genast traces this idea of relativism in literature back to the *Querelle des Anciens et des Modernes* in France in the late seventeenth century, and indicates that it passed on down through Voltaire to Herder. Naturally the latter interpretation

---

[1] Ernst Merian-Genast, "Voltaire und die Entwicklung der Weltliteratur" *Romanische Forschungen XL* (1927), 1-226.
[2] Op. cit., p. 5

of the term world literature is the one which has been chosen for this study of Herder's role in the development of comparative literature; and since the concept of relativism played such a crucial part in this development, an attempt will be made to ascertain to what extent Herder's views on the relativity of literary values are original and how much he owed to earlier writers. Furthermore the exact nature of this relativism, which has often been seriously misunderstood and misinterpreted, will be examined and some of the implications in the general study of literature discussed.

If comparatists are unable to agree on the matter of definitions they appear to be no less divided when it comes to evaluating the role of Herder in comparative literary studies. Some of the statements about him are so far off the mark as to make one wonder whether the critic in question was really familiar with his work; and some seem to cancel each other out by their contradictory nature. Two examples taken from basic handbooks in the field of comparative literature will serve to illustrate this point. H. M. Posnett in his work entitled '*Comparative Literature*' makes only two brief references to Herder, and in one of these he says:

> Yes; the ideal of world-literature, which Herder's Voices of the People did so much to foster in Germany, is attractive, especially to men who have never known true national unity. But, however deeply national literature may be indebted to international exchange of ideas, however splendid may be the conception of universal principles in literary production and criticism, the true makers of national literature are the actions and thoughts of the nation itself; the place of these can never be taken by the sympathies of a cultured class too wide to be national, or those of a central academy too refined to be provincial.[1]

In his somewhat cursory survey of the history of comparative literature P. Van Tieghem gives Herder short shrift.

> À l'étranger, un esprit tout nouveau soufflait avec Herder, principal représentant en Allemagne des idées préromantiques. Ce penseur, précurseur de Mme de Staël et de Taine, voulait retrouver dans toute poésie l'accent propre du peuple qui

[1] H. M. Posnett, *Comparative Literature* (New York, 1886), p. 345.

l'avait chantée; il annonçait l'histoire littéraire fondée sur la différence des génies et des races. Mais, nous allons le voir, ce chemin ne menait pas à la littérature comparée.[1]

A little further on Van Tieghem uses Taine as a whipping boy for Herder and criticizes him for ignoring *"influences"*.

> Il se montrait persuadé que la littérature est, comme la peinture, l'expression nécessaire de l'idéal et du tempérament d'une race donnée dans des circonstances données de lieu et de temps; et que les œuvres d'art sont d'autant plus significatives et d'autant plus parfaites qu'elles révèlent mieux cet idéal et ce tempérament, sans mélange d'éléments étrangers.[2]

By selective quotation one could make Herder out to be an extreme nationalist or an extreme internationalist, but one cannot have it both ways. In fact neither of these views gives an accurate picture of Herder's ideas about literature.

Yet many critics have been prepared to acknowledge the debt which comparative literature owes to Herder. George Saintsbury, whilst complaining about Herder's woolliness and failure ever "to compress and crystallize his ideas into a solid and fiery thunderbolt of literary expression", admits that:

> Stimulated by Hamann, by Lessing, and by his own soul, Herder betook himself, as nobody had done before him, to the comparative study of literature, to the appreciation of folksong (perhaps his best desert), to the examination of Ancient, Eastern, Foreign Literature in comparison with German. This is his great claim to consideration in the history of literature and of criticism: and it is so great a one that in general one is loath to cavil even at the most extravagant expressions of admiration that have been lavished upon him.[3]

Such praise is generous enough, but the critics generally appear to be most reluctant to go into any further detail than this. The reserve either

---

[1] Van Tieghem, *op. cit.*, p. 23
[2] *Ibid.*, p. 29.
[3] George Saintsbury, *A History of Criticism and Literary Taste in Europe*, 3 vols., (Edinburgh, 1900–04), III, 356.

6

takes the form of hedging warily, as with Joseph Texte: "Herder, qui pourrait bien être le véritable fondateur de la littérature comparée..."[1] – or of a bald statement, unsupported by evidence, as with R. Ergang: "He it was, indeed, who initiated the modern comparative study of literature, language, religion and art."[2] An article written by Louis Betz in 1901[3] does provide an exception to this rule, although the limited scope of the article compels him to stick to the bare outlines in his summary of Herder's position in comparative literature. Harold Jantz covers much the same ground as Betz in an article published in 1936, where he claims, "However, if any man deserves the name of father of Comparative Literature, it is Johann Gottfried Herder."[4]

More surprising than all this is the fact that a major study devoted to the life and work of Herder should omit any mention of comparative literature.[5] None of the familiar accounts of Herder's life and thought agrees with Saintsbury's assessment of his role in the history of literature. Even works dealing with Herder as a critic, such as those by Wedel[6] and Kohlschmidt,[7] fail to mention his contribution to the development of comparative literature. The more general works, which deal with the history of criticism appear in a more favorable light – both Sigmund von Lempicki[8] and Prof. Wellek[9] offer some useful observations about Herder as a critic– but there is hardly any attempt to examine Herder specifically as a comparatist. Lempicki says only: "Herders Verdienste

---

[1] Joseph Texte, *Études de littérature européenne* (Paris, 1898), p. 10.

[2] Robert Ergang, *Herder and the Foundations of German Nationalism* (New York, 1931), p. 109.

[3] Louis Betz, "Litteraturvergleichung," *Das Litterarische Echo* X (1901), 657-665.

[4] Harold Jantz, "The Fathers of Comparative Literature," *Books Abroad* x (1936), p. 402.

[5] Robert T. Clark, *Herder: His Life and Thought* (Berkeley, 1955). In an article entitled "Les diverses activités de Herder" in *Études Germaniques* XII (1957), pp. 312-330 S. Runacher also makes no mention of comparative literature.

[6] Max Wedel, *Herder als Kritiker* (Berlin, 1928).

[7] Werner Kohlschmidt, *Herder-Studien: Untersuchungen zu Herders Kritischem Stil und seinen literaturkritischen Grundeinsichten* (Berlin, 1929).

[8] Sigmund von Lempicki, *Geschichte der deutschen Literaturwissenschaft bis zum Ende des 18. Jahrhunderts* (Göttingen, 1920), pp. 360-414.

[9] René Wellek, *A History of Modern Criticism: 1750-1950*, vol. I (New Haven, 1955), pp. 181-200.

um die Begründung der vergleichenden Methode der Literaturforschung – als deren Sachwalter er oft gepriesen wird – sind darin zu suchen, dass er zuerst die Grenzen und Gefahren dieser Methode erkannt hatte."[1]

To be sure, the situation is not entirely negative. Alexander Gillies' article concerning Herder's preparation of Goethe's idea of 'Weltliteratur' provides a useful introduction to Herder's activities in the field of comparative literature, but a more precise evaluation of Herder's stature as a comparatist is really called for. It is to be hoped that the present examination of Herder's debt to his predecessors will shed some light upon this matter. Perhaps I should also state quite emphatically that this is not an attempt to provide the much desired history of comparative literature. Although there is much interesting material here my intention is altogether more modest and I have deliberately restricted myself to those literatures upon which Herder drew most freely. A more complete survey of the development of comparative literature and the idea of relativity would obviously, for example, have to take Italian criticism into account.

In order to bring this study within reasonable bounds attention is focussed upon a single body of Herder's writing, the seventh and eighth collections of the *Briefe zur Beförderung der Humanität*, published together in 1796. Such a decision may seem arbitrary and high-handed, especially in view of Saintsbury's complaints about Herder's works. Indeed the choice of text might itself appear eccentric when one considers Prof. Clark's curt observation: "Nor do the seventh and eighth collections (1796) bring anything new, although they are biographically interesting."[2] Evidently this last point refers to Herder's rather cool praise of his old friend Goethe in one of the letters. The seventh collection is considered as a mere copy of the prize essay *Ursachen des gesunknen Geschmacks bei den verschiednen Völkern, da er geblühet*, together with some remarks about hymns as folksongs and the piece on Provençal poetry, "the best part". "And the eighth is interesting today only because of its series of letters on form in art, containing a defense of German literature against the charge of formlessness."[2] Furthermore he claims that this aspect has

---

[1] Lempicki, *op. cit.*, p. 412.   [2] Clark, *op cit.*, p. 372.

already been dealt with in the *Philosophy of History*. Finally he delivers the 'coup de grâce': "If Herder were to be judged only by the last four collections of Letters for the Advancement of Humanity, his significance in the history of German civilization would be small indeed."[1] The list of those who have severely criticized the seventh and eighth collections includes the names of some of the most revered figures in German literature. Both Goethe and Schiller speak quite harshly about them in their correspondence,[2] and Friedrich Schlegel wrote an unfavourable review of them in 1797.[3]

Such a formidable body of severe criticism may appear most discouraging at first sight, but on closer inspection it becomes evident that the real target of the attacks is not any poor quality in Herder's style or presentation of ideas. Most of the critics simply disagree fundamentally with some of the ideas upon which the collections are constructed. The assertion about the lack of *new* ideas in the *Humanitätsbriefe* is, however, quite valid, and that is clearly the reason why Martin Schütze stopped short of these collections in his survey of the importance of Herder's works.[4] Yet he certainly does not dismiss them as worthless. They may well seem dull and repetitious to someone who has just read carefully through all the works written before 1796, but that is hardly a fair test for the value of the collections on their own. Prof. Wellek gives a more reasonable and correct estimate of their worth when he says: "One of the best of Herder's outlines is in the 7th and 8th collections of *Briefe zur Beförderung der Humanität*."[5] The lack of originality proves to be the strongest argument in favour of the use of these collections as a representative Herderian text. This is well illustrated in a statement made by Prof. Gillies in an article which reveals their great importance for Romantic theory:

[1] *Ibid.*, p. 381.

[2] Richard M. Meyer, ed., *Goethe und seine Freunde in Briefwechsel*, 3 vols. (Berlin 1909-11), II, 279-280 and III, 411.

[3] Friedrich Schlegel, 1794-1802. *Seine Prosaischen Jugendschriften*, hg. von J. Minor (Vienna, 1882) II, 41-48.

[4] Martin Schütze, "The Fundamental Ideas in Herder's Thought," *Modern Philology*, XVIII (1920-21), 65-78, 289-302; XIX (1921-1922), 113-130, 361-382; XXI (1923-24), 29-48, 113-132.

[5] Wellek, *op. cit.*, p. 198.

The *Humanitätsbriefe* combine older Herderian themes. The contrast between ancient and modern on historical lines, the idea of progressive development, in literature as in all else, the view of the merely relative value of each epoch, the consideration of the poet as an educator and evangelist, the consciousness of contemporary inadequacy, the belief in Germany's cultural future, the study of world literature in order to seek out its lessons, the new approach to the novel, the assertion that yearning, or striving after an ideal has developed in post-Classical times into a dominating modern characteristic-all these are points he had dealt with, in a greater or lesser degree, in earlier writings.[1]

The seventh and eighth collections do indeed contain all of Herder's essential ideas about comparative literature; ideas which he had put forward in many different works from the earliest essay *Über den Fleiss in mehreren gelehrten Sprachen* (1764) onwards. Sometimes the contents of such important works as *Über die Wirkung der Dichtkunst* and *Von Ähnlichkeit der mittleren englischen und deutschen Dichtkunst* are repeated almost word for word. An investigation of the principles contained in this work should produce a reasonably accurate outline of Herder's basic ideas for the study of comparative literature. An examination of the extent to which the ideas of the seventh and eighth collections had been anticipated in critical writings in France, England and Germany will provide firm evidence about the originality, or lack of it, in Herder's writings on comparative literature. Unfortunately it will not always be possible to ascertain whether Herder was familiar with some of the earlier works from other countries, but this should be no great disadvantage in a study of comparative literature according to the broader definition.

---

[1] A. Gillies, "Herder's Preparation of Romantic Theory," *Modern Language Review* XXXIX (1944), 256-7.

CHAPTER II

THE FRENCH CRITICS

Herder introduces the seventh collection of the *Humanitätsbriefe* with some remarks about the dispute between the *anciens* and the *modernes* in France during the reign of Louis XIV:

> In der *Cultur zum Schönen*, die wir der Kürze halben *Poesie* nennen wollen, springt uns der Unterschied alter und neuer Zeiten, d.e. der Griechen und Römer in Vergleich aller neueren Europäischen Völker, ins Auge. Wir mögen Italienische, Spanische, Französische, Englische, Deutsche Dichter, aus welchen Zeiten wir wollen, lesen, *der Unterschied ist unverkennbar.*[1]

The contrast between ancient and modern, classical and Christian writing looms large in the comparative historical survey of European literature in the seventh and eighth collections of the *Humanitätsbriefe*. Although the history of literary criticism in France has not been well documented[2] it is evident that the *querelle* is of great historical importance. In fact the origins of this dispute form a natural starting point for a historical survey, especially since they more or less coincide with another

---

[1] Johann Gottfried von Herder, *Sämmtliche Werke*, hg. Bernhard Suphan, 33 vols. (Berlin, 1877-1913), XVIII, 5. All further references in this study to Herder's work will be taken from this edition.

[2] The standard critical works for the period with which we are dealing are generally outdated, and limited in range. Auguste Bourgoin, *Les maîtres de la critique au XVIIe siècle* (Paris, 1889) suffers especially from these faults. More useful are: Ferdinand Brunetière, *L'Evolution des Genres dans l'Histoire de la Littérature*, tome I (Paris, 1890), Georges Ascoli, *La critique littéraire au XVIIe siècle* (Paris, 1937), and Saintsbury, *op. cit.* Pierre Moreau, *La Critique Littéraire en France* (Paris, 1960) is somewhat more limited in scope.

significant development. French writers began to use their own language rather than Latin.

The *querelle* actually began in Italy and it is difficult to establish exactly when it passed into France. Nevertheless one can hardly disagree with Hubert Gillot, who in his work devoted to the subject[1] considers Joachim Du Bellay's *La Deffence et Illustration de la Langue Françoyse* (1549) to be one of the earliest contributions to the debate. In fact it is remarkable that Herder and Du Bellay faced situations which were similar in more than one respect. The main purpose of Du Bellay's treatise is to persuade Frenchmen to write in their own language and to moderate an unduly respectful attitude towards the writers of Greece and Rome. One of his principal arguments is the assertion that no single language has a monopoly on culture and poetry, and that all languages are equally capable of development:

> A ce propos, je ne puis assez blamer la sotte arrogance et temerité d'aucuns de notre nation, qui n'etans riens moins que Grecz ou Latins, deprisent et rejetent d'un sourcil plus que stoique toutes choses ecrites en François: et ne me puys assez emerveiller de l'etrange opinion d'aucuns scavans, qui pensent que nostre vulgaire soit incapable de touts bonne lettres et erudition...[2]

In Herder's time veneration of the authors of antiquity was still quite strong; to be sure, the influence of French classicism was on the wane, but writers such as Lessing and Nicolai set great store by the writers of Greece and Rome. Lessing, for instance, disagreed with the French critics' interpretation of Aristotle but still accepted the basic authority of the Greek philosopher. In the *Humanitätsbriefe* Herder rejects the exclusive primacy of the ancients as strongly as Du Bellay. "Nicht in

---

[1] Hubert Gillot, *La Querelle des Anciens et des Modernes en France* (Nancy, 1914), 33 ff. The roots of the *Querelle* in the Renaissance period have been examined in two notable articles. August Buck, "Aus der Vorgeschichte der 'Querelle des Anciens et des Modernes' in Mittelalter und Renaissance," *Bibliothèque d'Humanisme et de Renaissance* XX (1958), pp. 527-541, and Hans Baron, "The Querelle des anciens et des modernes as a problem for renaissance scholarship," *Journal of the History of Ideas* XX (1959); pp. 3-22.

[2] Joachim Du Bellay, *La Deffence et Illustration de la Lanque Françoyse*, ed. Henri Chamard (Paris, 1948), pp. 13-14.

Athen und Rom allein wurden *dämonische, göttliche* Männer geboren."[1] He also chides those who write in Latin and despise the vernacular. A far greater problem, however, in his view, is the lack of respect which Germans feel for their own literature in comparison with other European literature, especially that of France. Like Du Bellay Herder is determined to uphold and improve the literary standards of his native country; this purpose is particularly evident in these collections of the *Humanitätsbriefe*. "So übel stehets nicht mit der Deutschen Muse, wie Sie fürchten. Es ist vielleicht der Hauptfehler unsrer Nation, dass sie aus zu grosser Gefälligkeit gegen Fremde sich selbst nicht kennet und achtet."[2]

In a modest way Du Bellay uses a comparison with another European language to make his point. Just as Herder uses the English as an example for the Germans – "Der poetische Himmel Britanniens hat mich erschreckt."[3] – so Du Bellay mentions the Italians as an example for the French. "Pour le sonnet donques tu as Petrarque et quelques modernes Italiens... marines à l'exemple de Sennazar, gentilhomme Nëapolitain."[4] And again he mentions Petrarch and Luigi Alamanni in connection with free verse. Yet these references to Italian literature do not alter the fact that the work is primarily nationalistic. Du Bellay appears to use the relativistic argument only as an excuse to promote French literature, and does not seem to be especially interested in its intrinsic merit. He does not attempt to investigate the special qualities which belong to the literature of each different nation.

Although Étienne Pasquier was a contemporary of Du Bellay the first complete edition of his *Recherches de la France* did not actually appear until 1611, four years before his death and many years after they were written. He expresses even more vehemently the ideas put forward by Du Bellay and attempts to prove by means of examples that the French language is as fine an instrument for literature as Latin. One chapter bears the heading, *Que notre langue Française n'est moins capable que la latine de beaux traits poétiques.* The following chapter provides a genuine example of a certain kind of comparative literature from the sixteenth

---

[1] Herder XVIII, p. 81.
[2] *Ibid.*, p. 111.
[3] Ibid.
[4] Du Bellay, *op. cit.*, pp. 122–4.

13

century. Pasquier takes various passages from Roman authors and sets beside them passages from French literature which are of almost identical content. The tone of his commentary on the texts is somewhat defensive, but at the same time firm.

Of even greater interest for comparatists is the chapter entitled *Si la poésie italienne a quelque avantage sur la française*. Using the same method as that which he uses in the chapter dealing with classical authors he brings forward numerous examples from French and Italian literature. He shows considerable restraint, neither claiming nor conceding too much for either party. Even when he places a poem by his old friend Ronsard above a comparable one by Ariosto he recognizes the danger of nationalistic bias: "Si une amitié que je porte à ma patrie ou à la mémoire de Ronsard ne me trompe, vous le voyez ici voler par-dessus les nues, et Arioste se contenter de rouler sans plus sur la terre."[1] At the end of the chapter he concludes that "Chaque langue a ses propriétés naïves et belles manières de parler, qui ne naissent point d'elles-mêmes, ains s'enrichissent avec le temps, quand elles sont cultivées par les beaux esprits."[2] The similarity of purpose between Du Bellay and Herder has already been pointed out, but perhaps the problems which faced Pasquier were even closer to those which faced Herder. At least Pasquier, like Herder and unlike Du Bellay, could point to some obvious achievements in his native tongue.

The importance of Pasquier's work goes beyond the mere comparison with Roman and Italian literature and encouragement of French literature. In the chapter *De la poésie provençale* he gives a brief account of Provençal poetry and stresses the importance of these works for European literature. "La fin de cette poésie fut le commencement de celle des Italiens."[3] And more precisely he speaks thus of Dante and Petrarch: "Je vous fais de propos délibéré mention de ces deux poëtes, pour avoir été les deux vraies fontaines de la poésie italienne, mais fontaines que prirent leurs sources de notre poésie provençale."[4] Herder's description of Provençal poetry in letter 84 follows much the same pattern; an

---

[1] *Œuvres choisies d'Étienne Pasquier*, ed. Léon Feugère, 2 vols. (Paris, 1849), II 48.
[2] *Ibid.*, p. 53.   [3] Ibid., p. 7.   [4] *Ibid.*

account of the various poetical forms, brief mention of some of the most distinguished practitioners of the art, with special attention being paid to members of royal houses, and a tribute to the profound influence upon the rest of European literature. There is no evidence to prove that Herder actually read Pasquier's work, but he acknowledges his debt to La Curne de Sainte-Palaye for information about the troubadours[1] and it is likely that Sainte-Palaye gleaned much from Pasquier.

The argument that each language is capable of literary development was really the only effective weapon for the proponents of the use of the vernacular in French literature. It was still being used by Deimier in his *L'Académie de L'Art Poétique* (1610). "…aussi chaque langage est propriétaire d'une douceur et galanterie de parler qui luy sont naturelles et aggreables."[2] Deimier was chiefly concerned with the form rather than the content of literature and his criticism centres on external features. "L'on prétend introduire dans la versification française les pieds et les mesures des vers grecs et latins, comme si la raison, la nature et l'usage de notre langue ne nous faisaient une loi de nous en tenir au principe des syllabes et de la rime."[3] Those whom he criticized in this manner were not, however, all conservative classicists. In the preface to his *La Sylvanire* (1627) Honoré D'Urfé stated that he wished to make France excel in Aristotelian unrhymed verse.[4] Yet the reason which he gives for attempting this is not imitation of the ancients, but simply more realism for the theatre.

Like Du Bellay before him he uses modern Italian literature for purposes of comparison; in adopting free unrhymed verse they disguised the fact that they were writing in verse, as the Greeks and Romans had done before them. In other respects D'Urfé strongly asserts the independence of French literature from the ancients, and his criticism goes beyond mere form.

---

[1] Herder XVIII, p. 34.
[2] Pierre de Deimier, *L'Académie de L'Art Poétique* (Paris, 1610).
[3] *Ibid.*
[4] Honoré D'Urfé, *La Sylvanire ou la Morte-Vive* (Paris, 1627), pp. 11-12.

15

Quant à ce que je n'ay pas imité la façon d'escrire de ces anciens Comiques et Tragiques, en la grande quantité des Sentences dont ils ont presque remply toutes leurs Scenes; je responds qu'en cela j'ay voulu suivre l'ordonnance des Sages, qui nous commandent de nous accomoder au temps...[1]

He goes on to point out how the ancients maintained a serious tone in their literature and suggests that contemporary kings and princes would not care for such Spartan fare. Poetry like everything else is subject to evolution, and he even sees a change in its purpose: whereas the ancients taught and by accident pleased, the moderns please and by accident teach.

This view of the role of literature in society was shared by François Ogier who declared in his preface to Jean de Schelandre's *Tyr et Sidon* (1628), "La poésie, et particulièrement celle qui est composée pour le théâtre, n'est faite que pour le plaisir et le divertissement..."[2] In this preface Ogier delves more deeply into the difference between classical and modern literature than Du Bellay, Deimier or D'Urfé had done. To begin with he takes the fight into the enemy camp by criticizing the classical rule limiting the action to a period of twenty-four hours, and complaining about the absurd coincidences which this necessitated upon the stage and the number of messengers. "De fait, c'est une chose importune qu'une mesme personne occupe tousjours le théâtre, et il est plus commode à une bonne hostellerie qu'il n'est convenable à une excellent tragédie d'y voir arriver incessament des messagers."[3] Yet he is not a militant unbending advocate of the moderns. He can see the essential difference between ancient and modern theatre and suggests reasons why the Greeks, and later the Romans observed the rules so strictly.

In the first place Ogier believes that Greek tragedies were really religious ceremonies and therefore the ritual was more or less sacred. This would also explain the absence of any violence on the stage. The second cause for extreme conservatism in the form and subject matter of ancient tragedies was the fact that the playwrights were always competing for a prize and were afraid that the juries would be unwilling to

[1] D'Urfé, *op. cit.*, pp. 17-18.
[2] *Ancien Théâtre François*, E. L. N. Viollet-le-Duc, ed., 10 vols. (Paris, 1854-7), viii, 13.
[3] Ibid.

accept anything that was original. The Romans, he declares, showed practically no originality and merely imitated the Greeks, doing little more than translating their works. Ogier continues with an interesting section on the relativity of taste among nations. Just as each nation has a different idea about beauty in women, "de mesme il ne faut point douter que les esprits des peuples n'ayent des inclinations bien differentes les uns des autres, et des sentiments tout dissemblables pour la beauté des choses spirituelles, telles qu'est la poësie..."[1] Ogier goes on to distinguish poetry carefully from philosophy, which is concerned with universal truths.

Those who slavishly copy the classics are specifically condemned:

> A cela il faut dire que les Grecs ont travaillé pour la Grèce, et ont réussi, au jugement des honnêtes gens de leur temps, et que nous les imiterons bien mieux si nous donnons quelque chose au genie de nostre pays et au goust de nostre langue..."[2]

Furthermore he realizes the full implications of this theory – people from different nations and periods of time cannot fully appreciate Greek literature, or any other apart from that of their own country and time. Speaking of Greek literature he says;

> On les regardoit en leur temps d'un autre biais que nous ne faisons à cette heure, et y observoit-on certaines graces qui nous sont cachées et pour la decouverte desquelles il faudroit avoir respiré l'air de l'Attique en naissant, et avoir esté nourri avec ces excellens hommes de l'ancienne Grèce."[3]

He proceeds to illustrate how this argument may be used in practice to justify the creation of a new form, the tragi-comedy, and once again the Italians are used for purposes of comparison.

Perhaps it is true, as Ernst Merian-Genast suggests,[4] that Ogier was only aiming at a defence of his friend's play without attacking the classics or offending their protagonists too gravely, but this short preface certainly has wider implications. I have quoted passages from it at some length because they present so explicitly and clearly the idea of relativity

---

[1] *Ancien Théâtre François*, p. 18.   [2] *Ibid.*
[3] *Ibid.*, p. 19.   [4] Merian-Genast, *op. cit.*, p. 39.

in literature at an early date. A century and a half later Herder expressed the same idea in words which resemble those used by Ogier. The theme recurs quite often throughout the seventh and eighth collections; two examples must suffice here.

> Wie ganzen Nationen Eine Sprache eigen ist, so sind ihnen auch gewisse Lieblings-gänge der Phantasie, Wendungen und Objecte der Gedanken, kurz ein *Genius* eigen, der sich, unbeschadet jeder einzelnen Verschiedenheit, in den beliebtesten Werken ihres Geistes und Herzens ausdruckt.[1]

The final letter of the eighth collection, which summarizes the results of Herder's investigations in the field of comparative literature, opens with these words: "Die Poesie ist ein Proteus unter den Völkern; sie ver-wandelt ihre Gestalt nach Sprache, Sitten, Gewohnheiten, nach dem Temperament und Klima, sogar nach dem Accent der Völker."[2] In the same letter, as in the first letter of the seventh collection, he makes some rather disparaging remarks about the value of the ideas brought forward by the conflict between the *anciens* and the *modernes*. In spite of the fact that all the French writers discussed so far must be considered as fore-runners of that conflict, they cannot be dismissed so lightly. Although, unfortunately, we do not have any external evidence to tell us whether Herder read the works of D'Urfé, Pasquier or Ogier, their ideas, espe-cially those of Ogier, clearly foreshadowed those of Herder in regard to the theory of relativity in literature.

As the rivalry between the two factions, ancients and moderns, mounted this principle was not actually denied, but was forced gradually into the background. The partisans of the moderns, in particular, used the idea of relativity in a nationalistic cause. According to them there was no reason why the glories of French literature should not equal the achievements of Greece and Rome. What is perhaps more surprising is the fact that even the most ardent defenders of the ancients did not abandon the theory. Merian-Genast deals with the latter group in some detail, paying special attention to Boileau, Callières and Bouhours. The principles and attitude of those who supported the *anciens* are probably

---

[1] Herder XVIII, p. 58.   [2] *Ibid.*, p. 134.

summarized more comprehensively and characteristically than anywhere else in P. Rapin's *Réflexions sur la poétique d'Aristote et sur les ouvrages des poètes anciens et modernes*. Published in 1675 this work has received little critical attention and is only briefly mentioned by Merian-Genast. The title is slightly misleading, since the modern writers receive quite cavalier treatment; indeed Rapin declares at the beginning of the first volume that there are only eight writers whom he knows, who really deserve careful consideration. Six of them are Greeks and two Romans.

The entire first volume is devoted to comparisons of these classical authors. Aristotle is singled out for special praise – regarding his rules Rapin says: "On ne va pas à la perfection que par ces règles et on s'égare dès qu'on ne les suit pas. Dans quelles fautes ne sont pas tombés la plupart des poètes espagnols ou italiens pour les avoir ignorées?"[1] The message is repeated throughout the work. At the beginning of the second volume, however, we find the statement: "Car l'Eloquence peut regner par tout, quand elle est véritable, et qu'elle a de quoy se faire écouter."[2] Rapin supports this suggestion that the ancients did not necessarily enjoy a monopoly in literature when he says: "Il y a encore des beautez et des ornemens dont chaque Langue est capable, que le poëte doit sentir, et qu'il ne doit pas confondre, quand il écrit dans une autre Langue que ceux qu'il se propose pour modèles."[3] This sounds quite similar to the position held by Ogier and his predecessors, but in his criticism Rapin appears to ignore completely the practical implications of his theoretical observation. This becomes abundantly clear when he speaks about modern literature; as in the cases previously mentioned the Italians are generally taken to serve as an example, but invariably here in a pejorative manner. When compared with the classics they are always found to be at a disadvantage. Their efforts at epic poetry are scorned because they do not fit into the classical pattern, and Ariosto is damned with faint praise: "Arioste a je ne sçai quoi du Poëme Epique plus que les autres: parce qu'il avoit lû Homere et Virgile."[4]

As one reads through the work one gains the impression that modern

[1] René Rapin, Œuvres, 3 vols. (The Hague, 1725), II, p. 105.
[2] *Ibid.*, II, p. 3.   [3] *Ibid.*, II, p. 152.
[4] *Ibid.*, II, p. 178.

authors really cannot do anything right, in spite of Rapin's lip service to the theory of equal opportunity. He praises the classical authors for their ability to write either in a grand style with plenty of metaphors or in the simplest tones when the occasion called for it. In contrast he takes modern Italian literature: "Arioste a trop de feu; Dante n'en a pas assez. Bocace a l'esprit juste, mais sans étenduë: le Chevalier Marin a de l'étenduë, mais sans justesse."[1] Nor does modern French literature escape censure, even though Rapin, like most other critics of the time, both *anciens* and *modernes*, shows an attitude verging on jingoism. Occasionally this must even appear comical to a modern reader; speaking of the tragic theatre he grants no more than half a page to the moderns and his comparison between English and French tragedy consists of the following statement: "Les Anglois nos voisins aiment le sang, dans leur jeux, par la qualité de leur temperament; ce sont des insulaires, separez du reste des hommes: nous sommes plus humains."[2] Further on he admits that the English are probably the people who have the most talent for tragedy, because the nation "se plaît aux choses atroces"[3]; but lest there should be any misunderstanding he immediately adds that the French people have applied themselves better to the task of developing and refining their theatre.

Unfortunately this lack of a cosmopolitan spirit was no less characteristic of the *modernes* than of the *anciens*. As Texte demonstrates,[4] the quarrel was really one between Rome and Paris. Charles Perrault, the chief standard bearer of the moderns, would have been much astonished if the name of Spenser or Milton had been introduced into the discussion. Merian-Genast insists that Perrault helped to keep alive the theory of relativity in literature; indeed he goes so far as to say: "Er hat diese Waffe geschmiedet, ohne ihren rechten Gebrauch zu ahnen."[5] Actually Perrault did not bring forward any new arguments on the subject; a glance at his main line of reasoning reveals that he merely followed in the footsteps of the critics already mentioned.

[1] *Ibid.*, II, p. 110.   [2] *Ibid.*, II, p. 186.
[3] *Ibid.*, II, p. 194.
[4] Joseph Texte, *Jean-Jacques Rousseau and the Cosmopolitan Spirit in Literature*, trans J. W. Matthews (London, 1899), pp. 12-13.   [5] Merian-Genast, *op. cit.*, p. 44.

Imiter les anciens n'est pas dire ce qu'ils ont dit, mais dire les choses de la manière qu'ils les ont dites; les anciens ont employé dans leur poésies les Fables qui étaient connues de tous ceux de leur siècle comme faisant la meilleure partie de leur religion; si nos poètes veulent faire comme les anciens, il faut qu'ils mettent dans leurs poésies ce qui est connu de tous ceux du siècle où nous sommes, et comme les poètes grecs et latins n'employaient point dans leurs ouvrages la mythologie des Egyptiens, les poètes français ne doivent point employer les fables des Romains et Grecs, s'ils ont envie de les prendre pour leurs modèles.[1]

Perrault certainly provides quite a comprehensive summary of the arguments in favour of relativity up to that time, but it is in vain that we look to the *modernes* for new ideas about comparative literature. Charles de Saint-Évremond, however, who spent much of his long life in exile in England did not get deeply embroiled in the *querelle*. In his works we find the genuine beginnings of comparison among the literatures of various modern European nations. In a series of essays devoted to the study of literature in general he goes far beyond the narrow rule-bound criticism of both the *anciens* and the *modernes*. In the essay entitled *De la tragédie ancienne et moderne* we find a statement which may appear innocuous enough today, but which was a bold one for a writer to make in 1672: "Il faut convenir que la *Poétique* d'Aristote est un excellent ouvrage: cependant il n'y a rien d'assez parfait pour régler toutes les nations et tous les siècles."[2] Wellek believes, not without reason, that one of Herder's greatest contributions to literary criticism was the role he played in the overthrow of neoclassical ideals.[3] To be sure, he was generally in sympathy with the spirit of the opinion expressed by Saint-Évremond: "So manchen Maasstab der Dichter Einer Nation oder verschiedener Völker man aufgestellt hat, so manche vergebliche Arbeit hat man übernommen."[4] Yet even Herder retains a reverent attitude before the Greeks in spite of his firm belief in relativity and his hatred of 'Rangordnung'. In comparison with Saint-Évremond he voices a thoroughly conservative opinion about Aristotle's *Poetics:*

---

[1] Charles Perrault, *Parallèle des Anciens et des Modernes*, 4 vols. (Munich, 1964), IV, p. 315.
[2] *Œuvres mêlées de Saint-Évremond*, ed. Charles Giraud, 3 vols. (Paris, 1865), II, p. 321.
[3] Wellek, *op. cit.*, pp. 181-182.
[4] Herder, XVIII, p. 135.

Ich getraue mich, in den Griechen jede reine menschliche Gesinnung, vielleicht im schönsten Maas und Ausdruck, aufzufinden; nur alles an Ort und Stelle, *Aristoteles* Poëtik hat *Fabel, Charaktere, Leidenschaften, Gesinnungen* unübertrefflich geordnet.[1]

Saint-Évremond continues his examination of the differences between classical and modern tragedy with a close look at the religious differences between the two cultures. He does not get bogged down by the numerous futile arguments of so many partisans of both the *anciens* and the *modernes:* instead we find a simple analysis of the situation. "L'esprit de notre religion est directement opposé à celui de la tragédie."[2] One by one he analyses the essential differences and demonstrates the theory of literary relativity in practice. Concerning the works of Sophocles and Euripides he says:

> Je ne dis point que ces tragédies n'aient eu ce qu'elles devoient avoir pour plaire au goût des Athéniens; mais qui pourroit traduire en françois, dans toute sa force, L'Œdipe même, ce chef-d'œuvre des anciens, j'ose assurer que rien au monde ne nous paroîtroit plus barbare, plus funeste, plus opposé aux vrais sentiments qu'on doit avoir.[3]

In a later essay, *Sur les tragédies* (1677), he casts a brief glance at French, Italian and English tragedy. He too cannot altogether escape the charge of chauvinism; few critics can, and Herder himself is sometimes guilty of it, perhaps because he regards it as a perfectly legitimate and natural stance to take. "Keiner Nation dörfen wirs also verargen, wenn sie vor allen andern *ihre* Dichter liebt und sie gegen fremde nicht hingeben möchte; sie sind ja *ihre* Dichter."[4] In this case, however, there are extenuating circumstances, since Saint-Évremond does criticize the French for the triviality of their plots compared with those of the English.

The comedies of the modern European nations are compared at greater length. Saint-Évremond establishes the fact that the essential difference between French and Spanish comedy stems from differences in social customs. Literature and society are clearly related to one another and certain features of society are used to explain corresponding trends

[1] *Ibid.*, p. 139.
[2] Saint-Évremond, *op. cit.*, II, p. 324.
[3] *Ibid.*, pp. 332-3.
[4] Herder XVIII, p. 136.

in literature. This represents an important new development in comparative literature which Herder was later to pursue most fruitfully. Saint-Évremond's knowledge of Italian and English literature is not particularly wide, but he recognizes his limitations in this respect and works well within them. Naturally he tends to stick to generalities rather than discuss particular works, but he still makes some illuminating remarks about the difference between the French and the English character, the consequences of which are reflected in the comedies of the two nations. Indeed, in this field he appears to be capable of rising above any national prejudice. His final judgement on the two outstanding representatives in this genre is significant:

> Notre Molière, à qui les anciens ont inspiré le bon esprit de la comédie, égale leur Ben Johnson (sic) à bien représenter les diverses humeurs et les différentes manières des hommes: l'un et l'autre conservant dans leur peintures un juste rapport avec le génie de leur nation.[1]

Here Saint-Évremond is using the same criterion of excellence in an author which Herder was later to use. In *Von Ähnlichkeit der mittleren englischen und deutschen Dichtkunst* and again in the *Humanitätsbriefe* Herder explains the greatness of Chaucer, Spenser and Shakespeare by demonstrating how they drew upon their knowledge of the British people and their folksongs.

Again and again Saint-Évremond returns to the theme of the difference between classical and modern literature, always laying great stress upon the role of religious belief in the creation of literature. The comparison between Greek and Christian literature is of more interest to him than comparison among various European literatures. Many of his predecessors and contemporaries were no less concerned with the contrast between ancient and modern, but none of them could view the matter with the same degree of impartiality. Evidently Herder shared his opinion that an understanding of the religious origins of modern European literature is essential before any worthwhile comparison between the works of the various nations can be attempted. The first portion of

[1] Saint-Évremond, *op. cit.*, II, p. 388.

the seventh collection is devoted to this topic and it recurs at the end of the eighth collection.

Certain other French critics showed an interest in the influence of external factors upon literature, but none of them went beyond the stage of a general theory. Fontenelle, who took the side of the *modernes* in the *Querelle*, declared in his *Digression sur les anciens et sur les modernes* (1688) that the oaks of the middle ages were no smaller than those of antiquity and that those of his own day were not inferior to those of the middle ages. From this he concluded that the French poets were capable of poetic achievements equal to those of the Greeks. According to his theory the only limiting factor for the production of great poetry was the climate. This interest in the influence of the climate on literary works was taken up again by the Abbé Dubos in his *Réflexions critiques sur la Poésie et sur la Peinture* (1719).

Dubos cites a passage from Fontenelle's *Digression* which contains the basic argument of Dubos' own work:

> Les différentes idées sont comme des plantes et des fleurs qui ne viennent pas également bien en toutes sortes de climats. Peut être notre terroir de France n'est-il pas propre pour les raisonnemens que font les Egyptiens, non plus que pour leurs Palmiers, et sans aller si loin, peut être que les Orangers qui ne viennent pas ici aussi facilement qu'en Italie, marquent-ils qu'on a en Italie un certain tour d'esprit que l'on n'a pas tout-à-fait semblable en France. Il est toujours sûr que par l'enchaînement et la dépendance réciproque qui est entre toutes les parties du monde materiel, les différences de climat qui se font sentir dans les plantes, doivent s'étendre jusques aux cerveaux et y faire quelque effet.[1]

Dubos sets himself the task of discovering why there is such a disparity between the artistic productions of different nations and different ages. Unfortunately he progresses little further than Fontenelle in offering an explanation. He reaches the general conclusion that the warm Southern climate favours the arts and he asserts that the liberal arts have never flourished outside Europe. He does not, however, enter into any specific details; he makes no attempt to illustrate how the writers of a

---

[1] Jean Dubos, *Réflexions critiques sur la Poésie et sur la Peinture*, 3 vols. (Paris, 1733), II, pp. 149-50.

particular European country were affected by the local climate. Nor did Montesquieu, who in his *De l'Esprit des Lois* (1748) followed Dubos in associating the temper of a people with the climate, come any closer to providing an analysis of European literature based on this theory. Apart from the ideas about the connection between geography and literature there is another reason why *Réflexions critiques sur la Poésie et sur la Peinture* should interest us. Dubos provides us with an early example of historical criticism in France. He defends Homer against some of the criticism levelled at him by the *modernes*, taking as an example Homer's treatment of horses. Dubos points out that man's attitude towards horses in Homer's time was completely different from the attitude of the seventeenth or eighteenth century. Referring to the manner in which Homer's heroes address their animals he says:

> Ces discours devoient plaire à des gens qui supposoient dans les animaux un degré de connoissance que nous ne leur accordons pas, et qui plusiers fois en avoient tenu de pareils à leurs chevaux. Si l'opinion qui donne aux bêtes une raison presque humaine est fausse ou non, ce n'est point l'affaire du Poete. Un Poete n'est pas fait pour purger son siecle des erreurs de Physique. Sa tâche est de faire des peintures fidelles des mœurs et des usages de son païs, pour rendre son imitation la plus approchante du vraisemblable qu'il lui est possible.[1]

Undoubtedly Herder was familiar with Dubos' ideas; he refers to Dubos on may occasions, and the indication to the *Réflexions* in letter 84 of the *Humanitätsbriefe* suggests that Herder read that work. Herder was not, however, greatly influenced by Dubos' writings, since he regarded the Frenchman as rather narrow-minded. The theory about the climate he found interesting enough in itself, but alone it was an insufficient explanation of the variations amongst the European peoples. He voices his objection to Dubos' one-sidedness in an article written in 1765:

> Montesquieu baut auf die Himmelsstriche und dü Bos rechnet nach Ausdünstungen der Erde. Uns dünkt, man hätte hiebey verfahren sollen, wie die Naturlehrer bey Erklärung der Ebbe und Fluth, die ausser dem Monde noch andere Nebenursachen, die Winde, den Boden der Meere, die Drehung der Erde um ihre Achse, dabey zu Hülfe nehmen.[2]

[1] Jean Dubos, *op. cit.*, II, p. 547.   [2] Herder, I, p. 88.

25

As Texte demonstrates,[1] there was an increasing awareness among Frenchmen of the existence of some sort of literary activity in other European lands, especially in England, after the revocation of the Edict of Nantes in 1685 had caused so many to go into exile. Yet there were few substantial comparative studies of modern literature. Béat de Muralt's *Lettres sur les Anglais et les Français et sur les voyages* (1725) did much to help the spread of cosmopolitanism, but unfortunately only one of the letters deals exclusively with literature, and more specifically with comedy. Following the example of Saint-Évremond he closely relates national character to literature, and he also chooses Molière and Ben Johnson (sic) as representatives, entering into somewaht more detailed analysis than his predecessor.

The familiar complaints about the lack of refinement and order in the English writers reappear, but Muralt lends new strength to the arguments by taking the concrete example of an English translation and adaptation of Molière's *L'Avare*. It is a pity that he limits himself to this single case, since this method proves to be most effective in illustrating national traits. Muralt makes one general observation about the differences between French and English literature which might profitably have been pursued further. "Les Caractères en France sont généraux et comprennent toute une espece de gens, au lieu qu'en Angleterre, chacun vivant à sa fantaisie, le Poete ne trouve presque des Caractères particuliers, qui sont en grand nombre, mais qui ne sçauroient faire un grand effet."[2] One might wish that Muralt had devoted more of his attention to literary matters. At least he shows us enough to prove that he was genuinely interested in comparison of modern European literatures on their own merits, without getting involved in any dispute between the ancients and the moderns or wishing to persuade us that the literature of any particular nation is superior to all others.

For a more complete survey of modern European letters we must turn to another temporary exile from France, a man who claimed that he introduced his countrymen to English literature. Of course there is

---

[1] Texte, *op. cit.*, 14 ff.

[2] Béat Louis de Muralt, *Lettres sur les Anglois et sur les François et sur les Voiages*, ed. Charles Gould (Paris, 1933), p. 116.

ample evidence in the writings of the critics already discussed to show that Voltaire's claim was somewhat exaggerated, but he never was a particularly modest person. Most of his ideas pertaining to the study of comparative literature are contained in two works – *An Essay on Epick Poetry* and the *Lettres philosophiques*. The origins of the former are unclear; it appeared in London, written in English, in 1727. Florence White asserts that Voltaire had a sufficient knowledge of the language by that time to compose such a work, but admits that considerable doubt remains about the measure of assistance which he may have received from an English friend. She comes to the conclusion that the essay was "essentially his own composition."[1] Six years later, after his return to France, Voltaire translated this work into French and made some important alterations in order to accomodate it better to the taste of the French public.

Both White and Merian-Genast attach great importance to the fact that Voltaire wrote the essay with an ulterior motive; to build up publicity for his own epic poem *La Henriade* which was about to appear in a subscribed edition in England. Certainly this factor must be taken into account, and it must have affected many of his arguments, but it is only fair to add that few of the works of comparative literature which we are dealing with in this study are completely free from some kind of bias. Ever Herder was not writing in a totally objective or disinterested spirit when he composed the seventh and eighth collections. The later letters, from 101 onwards, take on a distinctly hortatory tone in regard to German literature, sometimes at the expense of the literature of other nations.

Voltaire's essay provides the first systematic survey of any single genre in modern European literature. The most interesting section for our purposes is the first one, which sets out the principles upon which the essay is supposed to be based. The theory of the relative value of national literatures is firmly established. Likening poetry to a "suit of cloaths" he says: "If I am to give a Definition of a Suit of Cloaths I ought not to describe any particular one. Neither the *Roman* nor the *Greek*, nor the

[1] Florence D. White, *Voltaire's Essay on Epic Poetry. A Study and Edition* (Albany N.Y., 1915), p. 23.

French ought to be set up for a Pattern."[1] To prove that "there is such a Thing as a National Taste" he takes an image from Milton's works and compares it with a similar image in the works of Antonio de Solis, a Spanish writer, and then adds the comment: "Such daring Thoughts would be look'd upon as Nonsense by a *French* Critick, whose Exactness is often call'd in *England* Timidity."[2]

All the statements about the validity of national taste are, however, slightly misleading. In practice Voltaire was quite intolerant in matters of taste; despite the rejection of all rules at the beginning of the essay he adds certain qualifications. "An *Epick* Poem ought to be grounded upon Judgement, and embellish'd by Imagination; what belongs to good sense, belongs to all the Nations of the World."[3] Furthermore he lays down the requirement that there should be unity of action, and that the action should be "great, interesting and entire."[4] In a manner quite similar to that which has already been mentioned in the case of Herder he acknowledges the special position of honour occupied by the ancient Greeks and Romans. Indeed, he makes the bias quite explicit when he roundly declares: "The best modern Writers have mix'd the Taste of their Country, with that of the Ancients."[5] Thus the theoretical part of the work is slightly confusing. At one moment Voltaire states that there can be no universal rules and at the next he promulgates various rules of his own. Such contradictory statements continue throughout the essay.

Sometimes Voltaire appears to be taking a relativistic stand almost identical to that which was later to be taken by Herder and at other times he completely reverses his position and becomes quite dogmatic. One striking example must suffice to illustrate this point. As has been demonstrated already in connection with Herder's work, a necessary corollary of the relativistic view of literature is the undesirability of 'Rangordnung'. At the end of his chapter on Camoens Voltaire makes an observation which is quite in keeping with this theory: "...we must only conclude, that Wit is of the Growth of every country."[6] A few lines further on he opens the chapter on Tasso with the following com-

---

[1] White, *op. cit.*, p. 82.　　　　　[2] *Ibid.*, p. 86.
[3] *Ibid.*, p. 83.　　　　　[4] *Ibid.*, p. 84.
[5] *Ibid.*　　　　　[6] *Ibid.*, p. 112.

parison: "He us'd to say that the only Rival he fear'd in *Europe* was *Camouens*. His Fear (if sincere) was very illgrounded; for he was as far superior to him, as that *Portugese* excell'd the poets of his own Country." In the *Essay on Epick Poetry* we find the same sort of discrepancies between theory and practice as those which occur in the *Humanitätsbriefe*. Both Voltaire and Herder rank authors one above the other regardless of national differences in spite of the fact that both of them professed belief in the idea of relativity. Unlike Voltaire, however, Herder was aware of his nationalistic bias and considered it to be an inevitable factor in his criticism. Ultimately there can be little doubt that Voltaire's purpose in comparing the various authors of epic poems was not the same as Herder's. A remark in the chapter on Milton gives us a clue to his true intentions – a remark which in the French translation of the essay was removed to the introductory section:

> Would each Nation attend a little more than they do, to the Taste and the Manners of their respective Neighbours, perhaps a general good Taste might diffuse itself through all *Europe* from such an intercourse of Learning, and from that useful Exchange of Observations.[1]

Voltaire goes on to explain how the English stage might be improved by learning from the French and vice versa. Any such drive towards uniformity in European literature completely denies the validity of the doctrine that each national literature is a law unto itself, with its own special qualities suited to the people and conditions of each nation. Occasionally Herder also appears to undermine his own theory of relativity. In letter 101 of the *Humanitätsbriefe* he suggests that the Germans could achieve greatness by imitating the best traits of other nations:

> Wenn wir von allen Völkern ihr *Bestes* uns eigen machten: so wären wir unter ihnen das, *was der Mensch gegen alle die Neben- und Mitgeschöpfe ist, von denen er Künste gelernt hat.* Er kam zuletzt, sah Jedem seine Art ab, und übertrift oder regiert sie alle.[2]

---

[1] White, *op. cit.*, p. 135.   [2] Herder, XVIII, p. 113.

In the seventh collection and in the first part of the eighth, however, Herder respects national differences more truly than ever Voltaire did. The tendency towards international literary uniformity becomes more evident in the *Discours sur la Tragédie* which served as a preface to his play *Brutus* (1729). It contains a list of those things which Voltaire admired in Shakespeare and disliked in the French theatre, and more or less amounts to a programme for reform. Indeed, one point which he makes did eventually bring practical results on the French stage: he repeats the familiar complaint about the lack of action in French tragedies and offers an explanation. The fact that spectators actually sat on benches around the stage considerably hampered the movement of the actors and Voltaire launched a successful campaign to have the spectators removed. The other reforms were somewhat less felicitous. He tried to incorporate in his own dramas those aspects of Shakespeare's works which he admired. Hence the thoroughly unclassical and slightly out-of-place crowd scenes in *La Mort de César* and the rather contrived appearance of the ghost of King Ninus in *Sémiramis*.

The *Lettres Philosophiques* contain much interesting gossip about English writers, but the only letter with which we really need to concern ourselves here is the eighteenth – *Sur la tragédie*. In it we find a summary of the qualities and defects of Shakespeare and the English theatre in general. "C'est dans ces morceaux détachés que les tragiques anglais ont jusqu'ici excellé; leurs pièces, presque toutes barbares, dépourvues de bienséance, d'ordre, de vraisemblance, ont des lueurs étonnantes au milieu de cette nuit."[1] He even recognizes that Addison's *Cato*, "une pièce raisonnable", is spoiled by an insipid love intrigue which ultimately derives from the French theatre. "La coutume d'introduire de l'amour à tort et à travers dans les ouvrages dramatiques passa de Paris à Londres vers l'an 1660 avec nos rubans et nos perruques."[2] The final sentence of this letter proves that Voltaire had not yet abandoned his belief in the relative value of each national literature. "Le génie poétique des Anglais ressemble jusqu'à présent à un arbre touffu planté par la nature, jetant au hasard mille rameaux, et croissant inégalement et avec force; il meurt, si

[1] François-Marie Arouët de Voltaire, *Œuvres complètes*, ed. L. Moland, 52 vols. (Paris, 1877-85), XXII, pp. 152-3.　　[2] *Ibid.*, p. 155.

vous voulez forcer sa nature et le tailler en arbre des jardins de Marly."[1]

As he advanced in years, however, Voltaire became more and more reactionary in his views. His kind words for Shakespeare and Milton had been only too well received; in France during the eighteenth century interest in English literature increased greatly. Many translations appeared and some people even began to prefer Shakespeare to Corneille and Racine. Realizing that he had perhaps even created a serious threat to his own literary reputation he gradually ceased to mention the fine qualities of the English writers and deliberately emphasized their faults. At least according to his own standards they were flaws, and there was no longer any question of relativity. Already in the French translation of the *Essay on Epick Poetry* Milton received much less favourable treatment than in the original version, and as the years went by Voltaire became ever more bitter. The situation reached a climax in 1776 when he wrote the famous letter to the French Academy, by which time all pretence of adherence to the theory of literary relativity had been cast aside. Suffice it to say that this scurrilous attack on Shakespeare is in the very worst tradition of literary nationalism, completely negates some of the ideas expressed in the *Essay on Epick Poetry*, and represents an ugly stain on the name of Voltaire. Some of the criticism of Shakespeare had always been present in his commentaries, but he had still been able to provide useful ideas and material for the comparative study of modern European writing whilst he maintained some sense of the relativity of literary values.

Despite the reactionary views of his later years it is generally Voltaire who is taken as the sole propagator of literary relativism and cosmopolitanism in eighteenth century France: both White and Merian-Genast insist on this point. Yet there were others who concerned themselves with comparative literature, and one author in particular deserves more careful attention than the few sentences accorded to him by Merian-Genast. The *Essai sur le Goust* (1735) by Cartaud de la Villate consists of a survey of world literature from ancient Egypt down to the eighteenth century. For the most part it is not a particularly original work, but it is more comprehensive than any individual work by Voltaire, who never

[1] Voltaire, *op. cit.*, p. 156.

carried out his plan to write a survey of world literature. The early part of the work, which deals with the classical period in Greece and Rome, does not contain much material which could not be found in Rapin's *Réflexions*, but Villate does show a certain historical awareness. He recognizes, for example, the preeminence of the Greeks: throughout the era of French neo-classicism the Roman authors had generally been treated as the equals of the Greeks, and Voltaire even appears to esteem Virgil more highly than Homer.

Villate establishes the true relationship between Greece and Rome and shows how the Roman authors merely copied Greek models. He does not hesitate to declare that the comedies of Terence and Plautus were inferior to the Greek works from which they were derived. Nor does he fail to perceive the great importance of the spread of Christianity for European literature. He explains how a change in style was neccessary and how the early Christian writers initially stuck to a simple style. The failure to find a new style for the new subject matter led to certain absurdities. Villate cites the example of one Roman author: "Apolinaire, auteur de la Tragédie de Jesus-Christ souffrant, me paroît aussi ridicule dans ses personnages, qu'un homme qui mettroit du rouge et des mouches avec la triste décoration d'un grand deuil."[1] Although he comes no nearer to an explicit statement of the theory of literary relativity than the remark, "Chaque climat a ses penchans"[2], he seems to subscribe to it in practice. Generally he takes note of the various styles amongst different nations without passing judgement on them as Voltaire was wont to do in his later years.

Although we can be sure that Herder was familiar with many of Voltaire's works,[3] we have, unfortunately, no evidence to prove that

---

[1] N. Cartaud de la Villate, *Essai historique et philosophique sur le goût* (Amsterdam, 1735), p. 117.

[2] *Ibid.*, p. 163.

[3] Herder's works contain many references to Voltaire, including specific criticism of many of Voltaire's works. The most complete assessment of Voltaire as a writer is to be found in *Auch eine Philosophie der Geschichte* (v, 582-3). Herder concedes him the title of "Der Schriftsteller *von hundert Jahren*, der ohne Zank und Widerspruch *wie ein Monarch* auf sein Jahrhundert gewürkt hat –," but he is also sharply critical of him for his "*Leichtsinn, Schwäche, Ungewissheit* und Kälte!"

he knew anything about Villate's work. There is, however, a definite resemblance between the path followed by Herder and that which Villate pursues, although Villate does not enter into nearly so many details. As we have already seen, the seventh collection opens with an account of the decline of classical literature (including some observations about the servile position of Rome in regard to Greece) and of the significance of the rise of Christianity. And just as the eighth collection contains separate analyses of the literature of several European nations, so Villate tries to characterize the various styles which suit some of the peoples of Europe. In some cases he is not very specific:

> Cette manière d'écrire si saillante, qui a tant de charmes pour un Italien, déconcerte la roideur d'un cerveau Allemand. Sa marche a de la pesanteur, et craint les moindres secousses. Se repliant avec embarras, les vûës fines et détournées lui échapent. En général les gens du Nord aiment un stile de détail et qui ne cahote point.[1]

On other occasions he provides a more penetrating analysis: thus he says of the Asian style (by Asian he in fact means Arabic or Middle Eastern): "Son stile imite le cours de ces grands fleuves qui ne quittent un lieu qu'après avoir baigné ses rives par mille replis sur lui-même."[2] He supports this statement with some observations about the "Asian" character and with an example taken from their literature. His estimate of the Spanish and Italian styles is less charitable than the opinion of Herder, but he follows essentially the same method in probing into the character and history of the peoples in order to explain the literature. For instance, he attributes the Spanish style to "la Cabale, Chevalerie et un faux goût de métaphysique," with the result that "Cette triple chimere démonta la tête des Espagnols, et les guinda sur un Phoebus incompréhensible."[3] Herder agrees about the influence of Christian knighthood, but rather than of cabbala and hollow metaphysics he speaks of pride and "Tiefsinn," and their resistance to Moorish influences during the long years of occupation. "Sie sind veredelte Araber; auch ihre Thorheit hat etwas Andächtiges und Erhabnes."[4]

[1] Villate, *op. cit.*, p. 170.   [2] *Ibid.*, p. 171.
[3] *Ibid.*, p. 175.   [4] Herder, xviii, p. 56.

33

Perhaps Villate is at his least original when he discusses English literature. He notes their "goût des pensées profondes"[1] and goes on to talk about the lack of the unities in the theatre; this section is definitely tinged with disapproval and Villate's apparent impartiality breaks down. The criticism is familiar and only the imagery is new: "...comparables en quelque sorte à des sauteurs qui ne peuvent se plier à une cadence régulière."[2] The same applies to his criticism of the individual authors: speaking of Milton he says: "Sa narration est coupée de parenteses qui forment des hiatus aussi incommodes dans les discours, que de larges tranchées le sont dans des chemins publics."[3] The arguments which he uses are similar to those used by Voltaire in the French translation of the *Essay on Epick Poetry*.

Despite continued and increasing interest in foreign, and particularly in English literature no further comparative critical works like those of Voltaire and Villate appeared in France in the second half of the eighteenth century. The next significant contribution of this sort was the work of Mme de Staël at the turn of the century. Authors such as Prévost, Diderot and Rousseau did much to bring English literature to the attention of the French public, and there were many journals which also did their part. Many English works were translated, including much of Shakespeare. Most of this activity, however, took the form of mere reports about the latest publications in England or the incorporation of English ideas in French literature. Perhaps one author, Louis Sébastien Mercier, merits a special mention for his cosmopolitan spirit, but his contributions to comparative literature are scattered throughout his works. There is no single significant piece and his greatest importance lies in his role as an intermediary between France and Germany.

In French criticism of the seventeenth and eighteenth centuries the argument in favour of literary relativity appears quite regularly. It is a standard device for justifying new departures in literature and for breaking free from long-established rigid rules. Many of the French critics attacked the supreme authority of the classical rules with varying degrees of severity: admittedly none of them completely rejected those rules, but

[1] Villate, *op. cit.*, p. 184.   [2] *Ibid.*, p. 187.   [3] *Ibid.*, p. 189.

34

neither did Herder. In the enthusiasm of their nationalism they asserted independence in literary matters for each nation and language. Furthermore, some of these French critics were clearly aware of the importance of religion in literature and attempted an investigation of the historical development from classical literature to Christian. A few even showed some interest in the literature of other European countries; the urge for comparative literature was already evident.

CHAPTER III

THE ENGLISH CRITICS

In this chapter we shall examine the roots of comparative literature in English criticism and trace its development down to 1760. We shall also include certain authors who were Herder's contemporaries but were definitely not influenced by his writings. The main features of this development will resemble quite closely those of the previous chapter; the rise of historical criticism and the growth of the idea of relativity in matters of literary taste. Fortunately the history of English criticism has been much better documented than that of French criticism, especially in the period with which we shall be dealing, the seventeenth and eighteenth centuries. Apart from the general works by Atkins, Spingarn, Bosker, Wellek and Saintsbury[1] there are many more specialized studies such as Nichol Smith's work on Shakespearean criticism in the eighteenth century.[2]

For our purposes the most useful of the latter group is *The Historical Point of View in English Literary Criticism from 1570-1770* by G. M. Miller, which gives a good outline of the subject without going into too much detail. As far as Herder's connection with English literature is concerned Miller declares: "It is a common-place now to point out the influence of English writers on Herder."[3] Such a statement was something

---

[1] J. W. H. Atkins, *English literary criticism: 17th and 18th centuries* (London, 1951). J. E. Spingarn, *Critical essays of the seventeenth century*, 3 vols. (Oxford, 1908), (with a useful introduction). A. Bosker, *Literary criticism in the age of Johnson*, 2nd ed. (Groningen, 1953). Wellek, *op. cit.* and Saintsbury, *op. cit.*

[2] D. Nichol Smith, *Eighteenth century essays on Shakespeare* (New York, 1962).

[3] G. M. Miller, *The Historical Point of View in English Literary Criticism from 1570-1770* (Heidelberg, 1913), p. 7.

short of the truth in 1911 and would still be so today. He goes on to mention Lambel's work on Blackwell and Herder, Hatch on Shaftesbury and Herder and Kind on Young and Herder. Yet the works of Lambel and Kind are extremely fragmentary and a full-scale study of Herder's connections with English literature is still lacking.[1] His interest in Shakespeare and Macpherson has been quite thoroughly documented but we will be chiefly concerned with authors other than these.

Miller believes that the first significant representative of historical criticism in England was Samuel Daniel, whose *A Defence of Ryme* appeared in 1603, but certain earlier works show that their authors were somehow aware of the possibility of a historical or relativistic approach towards criticism. None of these is more interesting than the preface to *Ane schort Treatise containing some reulis and cautelis to be observit in Scottis Poesie* by King James VI of Scotland, published in 1584. There we find the statement: "As for them that wrait of auld, lyke as the time is changeit sensyne, sa is the ordour of Poesie changeit."[2] He also asserts that there is a positive difference between the rules which might apply to English and to Scottish poetry. Miller considers that these two points are sufficient to rank him as the first critic writing in the English language "to bring definitely together two fundamental principles of the historical method: (1) that the literary standards of one nation cannot apply directly to the work of another; and (2) that in the same nation standards must vary from period to period."[3] However, these thoughts are not elaborated upon in the main body of the treatise and there is a similar lack of consistency and perseverance in this respect in all the other critics before Daniel.

Although *A Defence of Ryme* was written as a reply to a work by Campion dealing with English metrics it goes far beyond the original cause of dispute. Systematically Daniel sets out certain general principles of poetry.

---

[1] The only work devoted to the subject of Herder's knowledge of English literature, Luise Schork, "Herders Bekanntschaft mit der englischen Literatur," *Beiträge zur Erforschung der Sprache und Kultur Englands und Nordamerikas*, Beiheft, 1928, is limited in scope.

[2] *Elizabethan Critical Essays*, ed. G. Gregory Smith, 2 vols. (Oxford, 1959), I, p. 209.

[3] Miller, *op. cit.*, p. 51.

> Every language hath her proper number or measure fitted to use and delight, which Custome, intertaininge by the allowance of the Eare, doth indenize and make naturall.[1]

This is by no means an isolated statement. A few pages further on he explains:

> Suffer then the world to injoy that which it knowes, and what it likes: Seeing that whatsoever force of words doth moove, delight, and sway the affections of men, in what Scythian sorte soever it be disposed or uttered, that is true number, measure, eloquence, and the perfection of speach: which I said hath as many shapes as there be tongues or nations in the world...[2]

As we have already seen in connection with the French critics, Herder echoes precisely these thoughts in Letter 107 of the eighth collection which begins with the words: "Die Poesie ist ein Proteus unter den Völkern."[3] And Daniel goes on to criticize various aspects of Greek and Roman literature and questions the authority of the ancients for modern literature; and this a full quarter of a century before Ogier did the same in France. The attack upon the revered position of the ancients culminates in the following declaration:

> Me thinkes we should not so soone yeeld our consents captive to the authoritie of Antiquitie, unlesse we saw more reason; all our understandings are not to be built by the square of Greece and Italie. We are the children of nature as well as they; we are not so placed out of the way of judgement but that the same Sunne of Discretion shineth uppon us.[4]

Using this argument as his base, Daniel proceeds to defend the "Gothes, Vandales, and Langobards" and condemns as arrogant ignorance the opinion that they were merely barbarians. A summary of his case for these supposed barbarians is contained in Herder's words: "sie fühlten die Bedürfnisse der Nation, in welcher sie erzogen wurden, und kamen diesen zu Hülfe."[5]

---

[1] *Elizabethan Critical Essays*, II, p. 359.
[2] *Ibid.*, II, p. 363.
[3] Herder, XVIII, p. 134.
[4] *Elixabethan Critical Essays*, II, pp. 366–7.
[5] Herder, XVIII, p. 136.

There follows an impressive passage where Daniel takes up Campion's assertion that Europe was spiritually dead from the decline of the Roman Empire until the appearance of "Rewcline, Erasmus, and Moore." In reply he demonstrates a wide knowledge of mediaeval literature and considerable interest in Italian literature. Throughout the work Daniel clearly places himself in opposition to firm rules in poetry and appears to lean towards what we might call appreciative criticism. Nowhere is this more evident than in two statements near the end of the piece:

> But yet, notwithstanding, I must not out of mine owne daintinesse condemne this kinde of writing, which peradventure to another may seeme most delightfull.[1]
>
> But in these things, I say, I dare not take upon mee to teach that they ought to be so, in respect myselfe holds them to be so, or that I thinke it right: for indeed there is no right in these things that are continually in a wandring motion, carried with the violence of uncertaine likings, being but onely the time that gives them their power.[2]

Herder displays a similar reluctance to pass judgement on an author: "Das demüthigste Genie hasset Rangordnung und Vergleichung."[3] In fact there is a distinct tendency in both Daniel and Herder towards that form of extreme relativism in criticism which Wellek finds so stultifying.[4]

The significance of Daniel's position becomes all the more clear when one starts to look for similar trends in the other critics of the period. As we have already indicated, other works contain various isolated statements but there is nothing to compare with Daniel's consistent line of argument. Indeed, more than a century passed before another English writer made such strong utterances on the matter, and the first half of the seventeenth century is almost totally devoid of any works which might further the cause of relativistic or historical criticism. The only figure who is of any interest in this connection is Francis Bacon, and his contribution is not directly concerned with literary criticism. Miller quotes several passages from the English translation of *De Augmentis Scientiarum* (1623) to prove that Bacon was urging a study of literature which would take into account "the forces that determine its develop-

---

[1] *Elizabethan Critical Essays*, II., p. 382.   [2] *Ibid.*, p. 383.
[3] Herder, XVIII, p. 138.   [4] Wellek, *op. cit.*, p. 184.

ment – racial, physical, religious, political and social."[1] However, the evidence which Miller adduces is rather vague and the assertion that Bacon's remarks are "of prime importance" for the development of historical criticism appears to be an exaggeration.

During the second half of the seventeenth century the strict rules of neo-classicism, which were formulated in France, steadily gained ground in England, but not without stirring up some opposition. The tone of Howard's *Preface to Four New Plays* (1665) is unmistakably nationalistic; but as we have already noted[2] this is a common flaw in critics of the time and does not prevent them from bringing forward perfectly valid arguments. Howard attempts to explain the special circumstances which compelled the Greeks to keep physical action off the stage and declares that their limitations no longer apply; therefore the French theatre, which tries to abide by the ancient rules, is unnatural and forced. The Italian and the Spanish theatre are also subjected to some brief criticism. In the preface to *The Great Favourite*, published three years later, Howard goes somewhat further in his castigation of the rules. He methodically point out the logical weakness of the rules which generally were accepted as those of Aristotle. For instance, he claims that an actual elapsed time of two and a half hours is no more equal to twenty-four hours than it is to a thousand years, and the unities of place and action receive similar treatment.

The abandonment of all rules leads Howard towards a critical position close to that of Daniel, which, as we have observed, has a parallel in the works of Herder. This becomes quite explicit in the statement:

> ...nor do I condemn in the least any thing of what Nature soever that pleases, since nothing cou'd appear to me a ruder folly than to censure the satisfaction of others; I rather blame the unneccesary understanding of some that have labour'd to give strict rules to things that are not Mathematical...[3]

It should be added that Howard is not altogether consistent in the two prefaces. In the earlier work he condemned the genre of tragi-comedy

---

[1] Miller, *op. cit.*, p. 72.   [2] Cf. p. 22 above.
[3] Springarn, *op. cit.*, II, p. 279.

and in the later one he specifically withdrew from any such firm judgement. The fact that he was writing a preface for his own work should be taken into account.

Another writer of this period who strongly attacked the rigid rules of neo-classicism was Samuel Butler. Although we cannot be sure whether Herder knew his short piece *Upon Critics Who Judge of Modern Plays Precisely by the Rules of the Antients* (1678) we do know that Herder was familiar with *Hudibras*. He even quotes a few lines from the latter in Letter 86 of the *Humanitätsbriefe*.[1] As might be expected from the title, Butler has great fun at the expense of the critics and comes out strongly against the rules. The familiar argument in favour of relativity in criticism appears here:

> As if the Antique Laws of Tragedy
> Did with our own Municipall agree...
> An English Poet should be tryd b'his Peres
> And not by Pedants & Philosophers,
> Incompetent to Judge Poetique Fury,
> As Butchers are forbid to b'of a Jury;
> Beside the most Intollerable wrong,
> To try their matters in a Forrain Tongue.[2]

John Dryden, whose critical works show considerable inconsistency and were apparently influenced by his own position in regard to the court and what we might call the Establishment, on occasion displayed a similar impatience with neo-classical rules. His *Essay on Dramatic Poesy* (1668) is especially interesting, since it contains an extensive comparison of French and English drama: this represents the most significant piece of comparative literature in England which we have yet encountered. The essay takes the form of a debate between four fictitious characters: Lisideius speaks on behalf of the French theatre and Neander defends the English. Lisideius praises French dramatists for their adherence to the rule of the three unities and blames the English for the complexity of their plots and for their creation of tragi-comedies. Neander finds this

---

[1] Herder, XVIII, p. 43. [2] Springarn, *op. cit.*, II, pp. 279–80.

variety to be a source of great strength in the English drama and criticizes the French playwrights severely for the monotony and predictability of their plots. Although Dryden offers arguments on both sides of the question his sympathies generally appear to be with Neander and the English dramatists. He appears to be on the verge of relativism when he refers to the inordinate length of the "harangues" in French tragedies:

> I deny not but this may suit well enough with the French; for as we, who are a more sullen people, come to be diverted at our plays, so they, who are of an airy and gay temper, come thither to make themselves more serious: and this I conceive to be one reason, why comedies are more pleasing to us, and tragedies to them.[1]

Generally, however, he seems to believe that the literatures of different nations can be measured one against the other and ranked according to some ideal and thoroughly subjective standard.

An interest in or contribution towards comparative literature is not necessarily limited to those critics who rebelled against the rules. We have already seen an illustration of this fact in the chapter on the French critics. Despite his conservative attitude Rapin demonstrated some interest in the literature of other European countries. His English translator Thomas Rymer followed a similar bent. Much scorn and obloquy have been heaped upon Rymer: both Macaulay and Saintsbury consider him to have been "the worst critic that ever lived."[2] Consequently some of his genuine merits as a critic have been overlooked.

Rymer opens his preface to the translation of Rapin's *Reflections on Aristotle's Treatise of Poesie* (1674) with a firm statement of his position:

> Nor would the *modern Poets* blindly resign to this practice of the *Ancients*, were not the Reasons convincing and clear as any demonstration in *Mathematicks*.[3]

He then proceeds to examine Rapin's arguments concerning certain fundamental defects in Spanish, Italian and French literature and adds a few comments of his own about Arabic imagination. Rymer is strongly

[1] John Dryden, *Works*, ed. Sir Walter Scott, 18 vols. (London, 1808), xv, p. 341.
[2] Saintsbury, *op. cit.*, II, p. 391 ff.
[3] *The Critical Works of Thomas Rymer*, ed. Curt A. Zimansky (New Haven, 1956), p. 3.

imbued with the spirit of nationalism; Rapin had found that some of the faults in the literature of the nations mentioned above stemmed from their national character or their language. Until he reaches the remarks about England Rymer is entirely in agreement with Rapin. However, the assertion that the English have a particular aptitude for tragedy he "cannot allow of."[1] Indeed, in his defence of the English he implies that it is not legitimate to judge a people by its literature, even though he has just assumed a connection between the two in the observations about the other nations. In any case he tries to shift the blame onto the authors rather than the audiences:

> Let our Tragedy-makers consider this, and examine whether it be the disposition of the People, or their own *Caprice* that brings this Censure on the best natur'd Nation under the Sun.[2]

The final section of the preface is of particular interest to students of comparative literature. Rymer attempts to prove the superiority of English poets by selecting a certain theme and examining the manner in which writers of different nations have dealt with it. Spingarn claims that "Rymer was the first Englishman to adopt this method of illustrating the poetic quality of the great works of the imagination by the treatment of set themes, and to add illustrations from the modern tongues: in this he furnishes an early example of comparative criticism."[3] The truth of the last remark is evident when we remember that Muralt's *Lettres sur les Anglais et les Français* did not appear until more than half a century later. Rymer chooses as his theme a description of night and cites passages from Apollonius, Virgil, Tasso, Marino, Chapelain, and LeMoyne, the latter being his favourite French epic poet. His comments on these authors are not always fair and he tends to cavil: for instance, he takes a couplet from LeMoyne:

> Aveque le sommeil le silence la suit,
> L'un amy du repos, l'autre ennemy du bruit.

[1] *Ibid.* [2] *Ibid.*, p. 4.
[3] Spingarn, *op. cit.*, I, p. lxv.

and makes the following observation. "The third Couplet is much-what as in a Bill of Fare:

Item – Beef and Mustard
That Friend to th' Stomach, this a Foe to th' Nose.[1]

When he has finished criticizing the efforts of foreign authors he unabashedly declares, "It now remains that our *English* be expos'd to the like impartial Censure."[2] He then proceeds to quote four lines from a work by Dryden and maintains their superiority over all the other extracts which have been discussed.[3] In spite of the marked nationalistic bias in Rymer's criticism one must regret that he, like Muralt, limited himself to one set of examples and left the reader "to judge of *Hercules* by his *foot*."[4] The preface to *Valentinian* contains a brief comparison between the work of Lord Rochester and Boileau, but this is only of minor importance.

A Short View of Tragedy (1693) is a somewhat disorganized work which does not contain much direct comparison between the poets of modern Europe. However, in the fifth chapter Rymer touches upon a subject which Herder investigated a century later. He stresses the debt which Petrarch and his contemporary Italian poets, and consequently all other European poets owe to "Provincial" poetry. He goes on to present a short account of Provençal literature and even suggests that it was influential upon Spanish literature, although he has already stated that the Arabs brought rhyming into Europe through Spain.[5] This matter is discussed more fully in the seventh collection of the *Humanitätsbriefe*. Scott Elledge gives Rymer credit for being "the first critic to relate early English poetry to the Provençal bards[6]" One should, however, remember that in France Pasquier had covered the same ground just as thoroughly a full century before Rymer.

The quarrel between the Ancients and the Moderns, which Herder alleged to have been of little benefit to European literature,[7] spread from

[1] Rymer, *op. cit.*, p. 15.   [2] *Ibid.*   [3] *Ibid.*
[4] *Ibid.*, p. 10.   [5] Rymer, *op. cit.*, p. 120.
[6] *Eighteenth Century Critical Essays*, ed. Scott Elledge, 2 vols. (Ithaca, 1961), II, p. 1156.
[7] Herder, XVIII, p. 5.

France to England. Although Herder did not believe that much good had come out of the *Querelle* Sir William Temple, one of the protagonists for the Ancients, had addressed himself to the great problem which Herder sets out at the beginning of the seventh collection of the *Humanitätsbriefe*. "Wie? kann man fragen, blühet diese schöne Blume der Humanität, *Poesie in Denkart, Sitten und Sprache* nicht überall und allezeit gleich glücklich?"[1] Although Temple is principally concerned in his *Essay on Ancient and Modern Learning* (1690) with a defence of the Ancients he conducts his argument in an objective manner and provides us with an early example of historical criticism. He does not merely assert that the Ancients were great; he tries to explain why they achieved what they did and why the Moderns do not measure up to them and does so by looking at the environment in which the various writers worked. Nor does he advocate slavish imitation of the Ancients by modern writers.

Temple's argument against the blind acceptance of rules rests upon the same base as that which Herder used. Both of them stress the overriding importance of genius in any writing which is to rise above the mediocre. In speaking of our debt to the Ancients Temple says:

> If these speculations should be true, [that Intellect is decided at birth] then I know not what advantages we can pretend to modern Knowledge, by any we receive from the Ancients. Nay, 'tis possible men may lose rather than gain by them, may lessen the Force and Growth of their own Genius by constraining and forming it upon that of others, may have less Knowledge of their own for contenting themselves with that of those before them.[2]

The same attitude towards all rules is evident in his essay *Of Poetry* (1690), and in this work he carries his interest in the historical approach towards criticism further. He tries to account for the powerful influence of "Gothick Runes" in all of European literature after the collapse of the Roman Empire and derives the word rhyme from rune. He also devotes quite a long passage to extolling the virtues of English drama compared to that of all other countries. He attributes this excellence to a unique English quality – Humour: and this in turn he considers to be derived

[1] Herder, xviii, p. 5.   [2] Spingarn, *op. cit.*, iii, p. 48.

from "the Native Plenty of our Soyl, the unequalness of our Clymat, as well as the Ease of our Government, and the Liberty of Professing Opinions and Factions...".[1] In thus accepting the importance of environmental factors in literature, Temple is well on the way towards adopting the idea of relativity in criticism.

George Farquhar's *A Discourse upon Comedy in Reference to the English Stage* (1702) provides a stronger and more concerted attack upon the Aristotelian rules than any which we have previously discussed. The tone of the piece is quite light-hearted, which is perhaps the reason why Miller dismisses it so casually ,but the intention is surely serious. After making considerable fun of the critics whom he characterizes as a small select group with no monopoly on sound reason he starts into his main argument:

> But in the first Place, I must beg you, Sir, to lay aside your Superstitious Veneration for Antiquity, and the usual Expressions on that Score; that the present Age is illiterate, or their taste is vitiated; that we live in the decay of Time, and the Dotage of the World is fall'n to our Share ...'Tis a mistake, Sir, the World was never more active or youthful, and true downright Sense was never more Universal than at this very Day; 'tis neither confin'd to one Nation in the World, nor to one part of a City, 'tis remarkable in *England* as well as *France*; and good genuine Reason is nourish'd by the Cold of *Swedeland* as by the Warmth of Italy...[2]

This statement indicates a more open-minded view of literature than that which was entertained by the partisans of the Moderns in the great Quarrel. As we have already noted,[3] Perrault and his allies mainly concerned themselves with a rivalry between Paris and Rome and paid little attention to the possibility of literary excellence in other nations. Hence Herder's disparaging comments about the Quarrel at the beginning of the seventh collection. Farquhar proves himself to be a genuine advocate of relativity; for him the truth of the adage "Die Poesie ist ein Proteus unter den Völkern" would have been manifest.

---

[1] Spingarn, *op. cit.*, III, p. 48.
[2] *Critical Essays of the Eighteenth Century 1700-1725*, W. H. Durham, ed. (New Haven, 1915), pp. 263-4.
[3] Cf. p. 20 above.

In the essay he demonstrates that the chief purpose of comedy is that "of schooling Mankind into better Manners". Having established this fact he draws the following conclusion: "Then without all Dispute, whatever means are most proper and expedient for compassing this End and Intention, they must be the *just Rules of Comedy*, and the *true Art of the Stage*."[1] He goes on to explain how an English play "is intended for the Use and Instruction of an English Audience." Since the English character differs from that of any other nation so the method of presentation must be unique, and he enters into a fairly detailed examination of the English "Complexion and Temperament."[2] "The Rules of English Comedy don't lie in the Compass of *Aristotle*, or his Followers, but in the Pit, Box, and Galleries."[3] There follows a section in which he launches a logical attack upon the unities of time and place similar to that which we have already seen in Howard, but even more sustained. In his introduction to this essay Durham claims that, "By its whole tone it shows that the opponents of free structure were in the minority, that they composed a complacent 'select circle', and that the popular taste of Queen Anne's time demanded from the drama essentially what we demand to-day."[4] This is perhaps assuming too much, but there can be no doubt that the neo-classical rules were coming under severe attack from certain quarters at the very beginning of the eighteenth century in England.

Another useful contribution to the Quarrel was Joseph Addison's *A Discourse on Ancient and Modern Learning*, published posthumously in 1737 and probably written about thirty years earlier. We cannot be sure whether Herder knew this work or not, but he certainly was familiar with some of Addison's writings. The third collection of the *Kritische Wälder* contains a detailed analysis of the *Dialogues upon the Usefulness of Ancient Medals*, and on several occasions Herder praised Addison's essays on Milton, although this does not necessarily mean that he had read all of them. The main ideas of *A Discourse on Ancient and Modern Learning* were later incorporated in the essays on Milton, and Hurd even suggests

---

[1] Durham, *op. cit.*, p. 275.   [2] *Ibid.*
[3] *Ibid.*, p. 277.   [4] Durham, *op. cit.*, p. xxxi.

this as a reason why the former "was not retouched, or at least finished by him."[1]

The purpose of the essay is to consider the qualities of the ancient writers which are lost to the modern reader and those which are gained through the removal in time. The first group includes allusions to living persons and contemporary works of literature and references to well-known and familiar places. The Ancients "lived as it were upon the spot, and within the verge of the poem."[2] The last circumstance which Addison mentions is the most important one for the purposes of this study. The Ancients had a knowledge of the "sound and harmony of their language, which the moderns have at present a very imperfect notion of."[3] Addison supports this argument with a statement of the principle of relativity which is so clear that it deserves to be quoted in full:

> We find, even in music, that different nations have different tastes of it, and those who most agree have some particular manner and graces proper to themselves, that are not so agreeable to a foreigner: whether or no it be that, as the temper of the climates varies, it causes an alteration in the animal spirits, and the organs of hearing; or as such passions reign most in such a country, so the sounds are most pleasing that most affect those passions; or that the sounds, which the ear has ever been most accustomed to, insensibly conform the secret texture of it to themselves, and wear in it such passages as are best fitted for their own reception; or, in the last place, that our national prejudice, and narrowness of mind, makes everything appear odd to us that is new and uncommon: whether any one, or all of these reasons may be looked upon as the cause, we find by certain experience, that what is tuneful in one country, is harsh and ungrateful in another. And if this consideration holds in musical sounds, it does much more in those that are articulate, because there is a greater variety of syllables than of notes, and the ear is more accustomed to speech than songs.[4]

Addison's arguments concerning the advantages which the Moderns may have over the Ancients need not detain us here. They all hinge upon the principle that familiarity may be the cause of disrespect in regard to the names of certain persons and places, and to various turns of speech

[1] Joseph Addison, *Works*, ed. R. Hurd, 6 vols. (London, 1890–91), v, p. 214.
[2] *Ibid.*, v, p. 219.   [3] *Ibid.*, v, p. 223.
[4] *Ibid.*

which might have seemed like *clichés* or too pompous to those who knew the language well.

In 1724 there appeared another determined attack upon the rules – Leonard Welsted's *A Dissertation Concerning the Perfection of the English Language*. Few of his arguments are new and we have already encountered most of them in dealing with Temple. "All that the ancients, or the moderns copying after them, have written on this scheme is no more than a set of very obvious thoughts and observations which every man of good sense naturally knows without being taught, and which never made a good poet or mended a bad one."[1] He complains that the rules touch only the externals of poetry without entering into the spirit of it, and consequently lays great emphasis upon genius as opposed to learning. The short passage which Welsted devotes to prose writing is of some interest since he makes a comparison between English and French style, using Addison and Fontenelle to illustrate his points. He claims that Addison copied the style of Fontenelle, which embodies those faults which were typical of modern French writers. The language was too refined and lacked vigour and Welsted deemed it to be "too imitable; that is, one easily sees through his art; one finds out the secret clue by which he conducts himself."[2] This is quite a reasonable criticism of the French neo-classical style.

This argument about the unsuitability of a highly refined language for great poetry is taken up by Thomas Blackwell, whose *Enquiry into the Life and Writings of Homer* appeared in 1735. Blackwell is rightly considered as one of the most important figures in the development of historical criticism in the eighteenth century and, as Haym points out,[3] Herder regarded him highly. The extent of Herder's admiration may be judged by an extract from the first collection of the *Fragmente* of 1766:

Thomas Blackwells *Untersuchung über das Leben und die Schriften Homers* (und leider! ist dies schäzzbare Buch, das in England so hoch aufgenommen ward, kaum halb ins Deutsche übersezzt); eine Untersuchung, die sich den hohen Sazz aufgibt: "welch ein Zusammenfluss von natürlichen Ursachen konnte den einzigen Homer

---

[1] Elledge, *op. cit.*, I, p. 326.　　　　[2] *Ibid.*, I, p. 341.

[3] R. Haym, *Herder nach seinem Leben und seinen Werken*, 2 vols. (Berlin, 1877-85), I, p. 139.

hervorbringen?" die diesen Sazz aus den Geheimnissen der Griechischen Litteratur und Geschichte mit wahrem kritischen Geist erklärt, und zum Homer ein Schlüssel ist – Diese Abhandlung sollte statt Einleitung seyn: eine Einleitung, die fast nie so nothwendig ist, als wenn wir uns dem ältesten, dem Göttlichsten, dem unübersezzbaren Homer nähern.[1]

Rejecting the possibility that there was "a miracle in the case" Blackwell sets out to account for the phenomenon of Homer. The basis for his study is the assumption "that a *concource* of *natural* causes conspired to produce and cultivate that mighty genius and gave him the noblest field to exercise it in that ever fell to the share of a poet."[2] The various circumstances are carefully analyzed. To begin with, Homer was a great poetical genius, a type much rarer in history than military or political geniuses. He was born in a particularly favourable climate amidst a people that was at just the right stage of development: sufficiently removed from barbaric customs, but not yet refined enough to have lost all their vigour. The language was likewise in an ideal state and the same argument is used for religion. Furthermore Homer arrived at a most propitious moment in history; Blackwell describes three distinct periods. "Greece was *peopled* in the First; she grew and the *Constitution* was settled in the Second; *she enjoyed it* in the Third and was in all her Glory."[3]

Homer is assumed to have been born during the transition period from the second to the third age. Thus he was sufficiently close in time to record the stimulating events of the violent early period without being caught up in them himself. We are even told that "...Homer's *being born poor, and living a stroling indigent Bard, was in relation to his Poetry, the greatest Happiness that cou'd befall him.*"[4] In the *Enquiry* Blackwell laid down certain principles with which Herder later agreed:

...we must remember that *young Minds* are apt to receive such strong Impressions from the Circumstances of the Country where they are born and bred that they

---

[1] Herder, I, pp. 289–90.
[2] Thomas Blackwell, *An Enquiry into the Life and Writings of Homer* (London, 1735), p. 4.
[3] *Ibid.*, p. 14.   [4] *Ibid.*, p. 103.

contract a mutual kind of Likeness to those Circumstances and bear the Marks of
the Course of Life through which they have passed.[1]

...I venture to affirm that a Poet describes nothing so happily, as what he has seen;
nor talks masterly, but in his native Language and proper Idiom; nor mimicks truly
other Manners, than those whose Originals he has practised and known.[2]

We find echoes of this belief in the powerful role of environment
throughout Herder's work. Nowhere is this clearer than in the concluding paragraphs of the eighth collection of the *Humanitätsbriefe*,
beginning with the statement: "Zu allen Zeiten war der Mensch der-
selbe; nur er äusserte sich jedesmal nach der Verfassung, in der er lebte."[3]
Yet despite his strong advocacy of the historical method in criticism and
his impatience with rules Blackwell did not go so far as Herder was to go
in supporting the idea of relativity. In the *Enquiry* he demonstrates that
all ages are not equally suitable for the production of great poetry.
"Neither indeed does it seem to be given to one and the same kingdom
to be thoroughly civilized and afford proper subjects for poetry."[4] Such
a sentiment is altogether out of accord with Herder's optimistic assertion,
"tendimus in Arcadiam, tendimus!"[5] In the opening section of the
seventh collection Herder posed the question:

Wie? kann man fragen, blühet diese schöne Blume der Humanität, *Poesie in Denkart,
Sitten und Sprache* nicht überall und allezeit gleich glücklich? Und wenn zu ihrem
Aufkommen ein besonderer Boden, eine eigene Pflege und Witterung gehöret;
welches ist dieser Boden, diese Witterung und Pflege?[6]

Blackwell had an answer to the second part of this question, and he
expressed the doubt that such ideal conditions as those which Homer
enjoyed would ever occur again. Despite his continuing admiration for
the Greeks Herder did not believe that any single period of history was
especially and exclusively suitable for the production of great literature.
Returning to the image of a flower at the end of the eighth collection
he says: "Flechte, Moos, Farrenkraut und die reichste Gewürzblume;
jedes blühet an seiner Stelle in *Gottes* Ordnung."[7]

[1] *Ibid.*, p. 11.   [2] *Ibid.*, p. 29.   [3] Herder, XVIII, p. 139.
[4] Blackwell, *op. cit.*, p. 26.   [5] Herder, XVIII, p. 140.   [6] *Ibid.*, XVIII, p. 5.
[7] *Ibid.*, XVIII, p. 138.

Certain other British critics appear also to have greatly impressed Herder, including the Warton brothers. Yet the frequent references to them in Herder's works are somewhat confusing; rarely does he specify which brother he is talking about and it is not always clear from the context. Indeed, we find in his review for the *Allgemeine deutsche Bibliothek* of Denis' translation of Ossian a remark which might lead us seriously to doubt whether Herder was really familiar at first hand with the work of either one of them. Summing up his arguments he declares: "Die Engländer haben also auch auf diesem Wege fast die schönsten Sachen zur Kritik erhalten. Warton über Pope und Spenser..."[1] Joseph Warton's *Essay on the Writings and Genius of Pope* appeared in 1756 and his younger brother Thomas' *Observations on the Fairy Queen* was published two years earlier. Yet Herder fails here to distinguish between the two.

Nevertheless there are some indications that Herder did in fact know these two works. In a 1766 review of *Briefe zur Bildung des Geschmacks: an einen jungen Herrn von Stande* by a certain Dusch he wrote:

> ...und bey den vorausgeschickten allgemeinen Einleitungen fanden wir hin und wieder ungenannte Auszüge aus *Wartons Versuch über Popens Genie:* wovon insonderheit im 3-5 Briefe bei Gelegenheit der Poetischen Historie sehr sichtbare und oft lächerliche Spuren vorkommen.[2]

Oddly enough this review preceded the other one by at least four years and in another review which dates from the same period as the Denis one Herder hints at his knowledge of Thomas' *Observations* when he speaks about "einen mehrern Auszug aus *Warton* über die *Fairy-Queen*."[3]

In any case, whether Herder knew Joseph's *Essay on Pope* or not (and it seems very likely that he did) it is an interesting document for the history of comparative literature in England. At the very beginning Warton proposes a historical approach to criticism: "We can never completely relish, or adequately understand any author, especially any Ancient, except we constantly keep in our eye his climate, his country,

---

[1] Herder, v, p. 330.   [2] *Ibid.*, 1 p. 115.
[3] *Ibid.*, v, p. 315.

and his age."[1] He goes on to criticize Pope for mixing elements from Greece with those of England. However, Warton is also by no means a straightforward supporter of the idea of relativity in criticism. In one passage he generously praises the achievements of French criticism and readily acknowledges the debt which the English critics owed to their French colleagues; but he still harks back to the authority of the Greeks. Speaking of the French critics he says: "...but that these are sufficient to form a taste upon, without having recourse to the genuine fountains of all polite literature, I mean the Grecian writers, no one but a superficial reader can allow."[2]

Joseph Warton certainly cannot be regarded as a defender of the rules. He seems to agree with Temple about the danger of true genius being smothered by the rules and adds his own observation: "In no polished nation, after criticism has been much studied, and the rules of writing established, has any very extraordinary work ever appeared."[3] Yet he generally tends to avoid formulating theories about literature and tries to stick to concrete examples. This attitude is spelt out clearly at the beginning of the second volume of the *Essay* when he states that: "Among the various causes however that have been assigned, why poetry and the arts have more eminently flourished in some particular ages and nations, than in others, few have been satisfactory and adequate."[4] And he leaves the matter to rest there.

Warton devotes a whole chapter to each of Pope's major works and is always ready to compare these works with examples from French, Italian or Spanish literature. The comparisons with French literature are much more frequent than those with the literature of any other nation, since that is where Warton's knowledge was most thorough. For instance, in the chapter dealing with Pope's lyric poetry he gives a brief survey of modern lyric poetry, mentioning the works of Petrarch, Metastasio, Boileau, Malherbe, LaMotte and Voltaire. Discussing *The Rape of the Lock*, Warton examines in some detail Tassoni's *La Secchia Rapita*, Boileau's *Le Lutrin*, and Garth's *The Dispensary*. Boileau's work

[1] Joseph Warton, *An Essay on the Genius and Writings of Pope*, 5th ed., 2 vols. (London, 1806), I, p. 5.
[2] *Ibid.*, I, pp. 197-8.   [3] *Ibid.*, I, p. 198.   [4] *Ibid.*, II, p. 23.

is brought under even closer scrutiny in connection with Pope's *Epistle to Dr. Arbuthnot*. The chapter on the *Essay on Man* is filled with comparisons, mostly from French literature. Warton shows how Pope derived many of his thoughts, either directly or indirectly, from such writers as Pascal, Montaigne, LaRochefoucauld, and Montesquieu, and he quotes quite fully Voltaire's remarks about the similarity of his own thoughts with those contained in the *Essay on Man*.

Thomas Warton's *Observations on the Fairy Queen*, which Herder also probably knew, is described by Miller as an "epoch-making work."[1] This is, perhaps, a slight exaggeration, but the work does represent an important stage in the development of historical criticism. Again it is the practical application of the method rather than any new contribution to theory which is the distinguishing feature. Several passages from the additions to the second edition of 1762 have been cited in an attempt to establish Warton as the founder of historical criticism. After making an interesting comparison between the works of Ariosto and Spenser he remarks:

> But it is absurd to think of judging either Ariosto or Spenser by precepts which they did not attend to. We who live in the days of writing by rule, are apt to try every composition by those laws which we have been taught to think the sole criterion of excellence. Critical taste is universally diffused, and we require the same order and design which every modern performance is expected to have, in poems where they never were regarded or intended.[2]

And at the beginning of the chapter dealing with Spenser's "Allegorical Character" we find the admonition:

> In reading the works of a poet who lived in a remote age, it is necessary that we should look back upon the customs and manners which prevailed in that age. We should endeavour to place ourselves in the writer's situation and circumstances. Hence we shall become better enabled to discover, how his turn of thinking, and manner of composing, were influenced by familiar appearances and established objects, which are utterly different from those with which we are at present surrounded.[3]

[1] Miller, *op. cit.*, p. 128.
[2] Thomas Warton, *Observations on the Fairy Queen of Spenser*, 2nd ed., 2 vols. (London, 1762), I, p. 15.   [3] *Ibid.*, II, p. 87.

We can see that these passages really do not contain any ideas which we have not already met with in earlier critics. Indeed, it has been pointed out on several occasions[1] that most of the first passage was lifted by Warton from John Hughes' preface to an edition of Spenser, published in 1715. In connection with the second passage Wellek makes the following comment:

> The second edition of the *Observations* contains evidence that Warton's interest in old literature had been newly fortified by the argument of "relativity". It shows the increase of historical tolerance in the age. In the 1754 edition, there was tolerance which was actually nothing new in itself.[2]

Ample evidence is available to show that the historical point of view had become more or less acceptable, even to neo-classicists, by the middle of the eighteenth century. Shortly after the first edition of the *Observations* was published Dr. Johnson himself wrote a letter to Warton commending him for his conscious efforts at historical criticism.[3] Even in his own *Preface to an Edition of Shakespeare* (1765) Johnson wrote: "Every man's performances, to be rightly estimated, must be compared with the state of the age in which he lived, and with his own particular opportunities."[4] Johnson, however, still did not accept completely the idea of relativity: in the same *Preface* he recognizes implicitly the supreme position of Aristotle. Thus in judging Shakespeare he says:

> He has not, indeed, an intrigue regularly perplexed and regularly unravelled:he does not endeavour to hide his design only to discover it, for this is seldom the order of real events, and *Shakespeare* is the poet of nature: But his plan has commonly what *Aristotle* requires, a beginning, a middle, and an end; one event is concatenated with another, and the conclusion follows by easy consequence.[5]

[1] Elledge, *op. cit.*, I, p. 544; and Odell Shepard's review of Clarissa Rinaker's *Thomas Warton* (Urbana, 1916) in JEGP, XVI (1917), p. 153 ff.
[2] René Wellek, *The Rise of English Literary History* (Chapel Hill, 1941), p. 168.
[3] Boswell's *Life of Johnson*, ed. G.P. Hill, rev. and enl. L. F. Powell, 6 vols. (Oxford, 1934-50), I, p. 270.
[4] Samuel Johnson, *Works*, 11 vols. (London, 1787), IX, p. 264.
[5] *Ibid.*, IX, p. 257.

Thomas Warton applied himself even more fully to historical criticism in his *History of English Poetry*, which was published in three volumes (1774, 1778 and 1781). We can be fairly sure that Herder was familiar with at least part of this work. In the eighth collection of the *Humanitäts-briefe* he includes it amongst "die schätzbarsten Produkten des Auslandes".[1] As Warton says in his preface, the *History* is not confined exclusively to the consideration of English poetry; quite frequently he stops along the way "for a comparative survey of the poetry of other nations."[2] For instance, when he examines Chaucer he feels obliged to give an account of Provençal poetry and of the state of Italian and French literature from which Chaucer derived so much. He delves quite deeply into the history and significance of Provençal poetry, using La Curne de Sainte-Palaye as one of his main sources.

In his survey of European literature in the seventh collection of the *Humanitätsbriefe* Herder also found it necessary to write at some length about the influence of the Provençal poets. He too relied upon La Curne de Sainte-Palaye for much of his information.[3] In the eighty-fifth letter he traces the stimulus for Provençal poetry back through Spain to the Arabs and stresses the debt which modern European literature owes to Arabic culture. "...gewiss, so sind wir ihnen wie in der Chemie und Arzneikunst so auch in der Dichtung viele *gebrannte Wasser* schuldig."[4] The important role of the Arabs in European letters also figures in Warton's preliminary dissertation to the *History of English Poetry*, entitled *Of the Origin of Romantic Fiction in Europe*. Herder makes a specific reference to this essay in *Ideen zur Philosophie der Geschichte der Menschheit*[5] and it seems quite likely that he culled some ideas from it. Warton had also traced the path of Arabic influences from Northern Africa, through Spain to France, rather than through the crusades; an opinion which was apparently quite common at the time when Warton was writing. And he had emphasized the tremendous power of the Arabs' imagination – "jene *Phantome Asiatischer Einbildungskraft*"[6] as Herder

[1] Herder, XVIII, p. 131.
[2] Thomas Warton, *The History of English Poetry*, 4 vols. (London, 1775-81), I, p. iv.
[3] Herder, XVIII, p. 34.   [4] *Ibid*, XVIII, p. 42.
[5] *Ibid*, XVI, p. 266.   [6] *Ibid*, XVIII, p. 42.

describes it when acknowledging its strong effect upon the European mind.

Many of the ideas of both Warton brothers reappear in Edward Young's *Conjectures on Original Composition* (1759). Despite his assertion at the beginning of the essay; "I begin with *Original* Composition; and the more willingly, as it seems an original subject to me, who have seen nothing hitherto written on it."[1] Young's thoughts were, ironically, far from original. The whole work is really no more than a long plea for the independence of genius from all rules and especially from the slavish imitation of the Ancients. A familiar enough theme, as we have already observed in this chapter. Yet the *Conjectures* were of more than passing significance for Herder. As Haym tells us: "Das Feuer dieser Schrift, die sich schon in Herders ältestem Arbeitsheft excerpirt findet, hatte ihm 'angeglüht'."[2] The strong argument that every original genius must develop his own natural talents appealed to Herder, who wished to see just such a development in Germany. This is already evident in the second collection of the *Fragmente* (1767) and there is little doubt that this was one of the motivating factors behind his survey of European literature in the *Humanitätsbriefe*.

Several other English writers of this period whom Herder esteemed launched strong attacks upon the rules, and the critics who abided by them. The opening chapter of each book in Henry Fielding's *Tom Jones* (1749) generally consists of critical observations. In Book v Chapter 1 he openly challenges the authority of the critics and proceeds to put them in their place.

> The critic, rightly considered, is no more than the clerk, whose office it is to tran-scribe the rules and laws laid down by those great judges whose vast strength of genius hath placed them in the light of legislators, in the several sciences over which they presided.[3]

Then there is the famous chapter in the third book of Laurence Sterne's

---

[1] Edward Young, *Conjectures on Original Composition*, ed. Edith J. Morley (Manchester, 1918), p. 4.

[2] Haym, *op. cit.*, I, p. 149.

[3] Henry Fielding, *Works*, ed. Leslie Stephens, 10 vols. (London, 1882), I, p. 184.

Tristram Shandy (1761), where he belabours the critics in a humorous fashion:

> ...their heads, Sir, are stuck so full of rules and compasses, and have that eternal propensity to apply them upon all occasions, that a work of genius had better go to the devil at once, than stand to be pricked and tortured to death by 'em.[1]

A more sustained attack comes in Oliver Goldsmith's *An Inquiry into the Present State of Polite Learning in Europe* (1759). This work, which bears such a promising title, is rather disappointing as far as comparative literature is concerned. Goldsmith mainly limits himself to general remarks about the character of the people of Italy, Germany, Holland, France and England. He rarely enters into detail about literary works. As far as the critics are concerned he clearly had an axe to grind. The first two chapters explain how the advance of criticism signals the decline of literary excellence. For our purposes the most interesting section of the work is the seventh chapter, which was omitted from the second edition. Goldsmith claims that "the polite learning" of England and France is "incapable of comparison" owing to a profound difference in national temperament. He concludes the chapter with a plea for relativity. "Critics should, therefore, imitate physicians, and consider every country as having a peculiar constitution, and consequently requiring a peculiar regimen."[2]

In the ninety-ninth letter of the *Humanitätsbriefe* Herder praises Fielding and Sterne, and judging by a reference in the third collection of the *Fragmente* it seems reasonable to assume that he read Tom Jones.[3] We certainly know that he read *Tristram Shandy*. Haym informs us that Sterne was one of Herder's favourite authors during the Riga period and Herder's correspondence definitely backs up such a claim. Harvey W. Hewett-Thayer cites passages from Herder's letters to Hamann and shows "that Shandy had so far forced its claims upon a little set of book-lovers in the remote east, Herder, Hamann and a few others, that they

---

[1] Laurence Sterne, *The Life and Opinions of Tristram Shandy, Gentleman*, ed. James A. Work (New York, 1940), p. 140.
[2] Oliver Goldsmith, *Works*, ed. Peter Cunningham, 4 vols. (London, 1854), II, p. 74.
[3] Herder, I, p. 516.

gave one another in play names from the English novel."[1] Herder's knowledge of Goldsmith's *Inquiry* is much less certain. Haym assures us: "Hoch in Gunst stand bei Herder ferner Oliver Goldsmith"[2]. But this surely only refers to *The Vicar of Wakefield* which he read together with Goethe in Strasbourg.

Richard Hurd's *Letters on Chivalry and Romance* brought a further practical application of the historical method in criticism. Hurd's personal position is thoroughly ambivalent; speaking of his knowledge of the "old Romances" in Letter IV he says:

> Not that I shall make a merit with you in having perused these barbarous volumes myself; much less would I impose the ungrateful task upon you. Thanks to the curiosity of certain painful collectors, this knowledge may be obtained at a cheaper rate.[3]

Nevertheless he accepts the idea of relativity sufficiently to enumerate "some few circumstances of agreement between the *heroic* and *gothic* manners."[4] And in Letter VIII he makes an unequivocal statement on the matter:

> When an architect examines a Gothic structure by Grecian rules, he finds nothing but deformity. But the Gothic architecture has it's own rules, by which when it comes to be examined, it is seen to have it's merit, as well as the Grecian. The question is not, which of the two is conducted in the simplest or truest taste: but, whether there be not sense and design in both, when scrutinized by the laws on which each is projected.[5]

Hurd goes on in the next letter to make a comparison between Spenser's *Fairy Queen* and Tasso's *Gerusalemme Liberata*. He criticizes Tasso for trying to "trim" between the Gothic and the classical model. The principle which Hurd lays down here is the same as that which Herder propounds in the *Humanitätsbriefe*. Herder makes many references to

[1] Harvey W. Hewett-Thayer, *Laurence Sterne in Germany*, Columbia University Germanic Studies, Vol. II, No. I, (New York, 1905), p. 28.
[2] Haym, *op. cit.*, I, p. 413.
[3] Richard Hurd, *Letters on Chivalry and Romance*, ed. Edith J. Morley (London, 1911), p. 94.
[4] *Ibid.*, p. 95.   [5] *Ibid.*, p. 118.

Hurd in his works, and a remark in *Von Ähnlichkeit der mittlern englischen und deutschen Dichtkunst*[1] clearly indicates that he had read the *Letters on Chivalry and Romance*.

In 1763 Dr. John Brown published his *Dissertation on the Rise, Union, and Power, the Progressions, Separations, and Corruptions of Poetry and Music*. His purpose is to show how music, dancing and poetry were all closely united in primitive society, and how they gradually drifted apart. In the final section he even tries to point the way towards a possible re-union. He sketches a history of poetry and music, devoting most of his attention to Greece and Rome. The sections dealing with "the polished Nations of Europe" and China, Peru and India are disappointingly brief, but Brown does make an attempt at comparing the development of poetry in Italy, France and England.

Herder was certainly familiar with this work. He makes two rather critical references to it; in the second of these he gives a summary of Brown's main hypothesis and adds the comment:

> Hätte er sich mit wahren Thatsachen begnügt und seine Meinung nicht auch auf Zeiten und Gegenstände ausgebreitet, wo sie nicht mehr statt findet, hätte er insonderheit die Gesetzgeber aus dem Spiel gelassen, und nicht Alles in jeder Art der Dichtkunst aus ihr erklären wollen: so wüsste ich nicht, was man ihm entgegen setzen könnte?[2]

In the seventh collection of the *Humanitätsbriefe* he in fact stresses the importance of the union of music and poetry, and examines the consequences of the split between them more thoroughly than Brown had done.

We have now reached a period, the mid 1760's, which marks the beginning of Herder's activity in the literary world. As has already been pointed out, the *Humanitätsbriefe* contain many ideas which had been expressed in earlier works, some of them even dating back to the first collection of the *Fragmente*. Therefore it would be hazardous to suggest that any works which appeared in England after 1765 had a direct influence upon the *Humanitätsbriefe* and Herder's ideas about comparative

[1] Herder, IX, p. 523.   [2] *Ibid.*, XII, p. 177.

literature. On the other hand one can be reasonably sure that none of the three remaining authors to be discussed was influenced in any way by Herder's works. There is no evidence that any of them knew anything about him; indeed there is no reason to suppose that they had any knowledge of the German language – a necessary requirement for the study of Herder's writings before 1800. What we shall be dealing with, therefore, are contributions to comparative literature parallel to those of Herder.

In 1783 Dr. Hugh Blair retired from his Regius Professorship at Edinburgh University and published the lectures which he had given during the previous two decades, under the title *Lectures on Rhetoric and Belles Lettres*. Much of this work is devoted to grammar and the practical matter of writing and speaking in public in a correct manner. Blair devotes much space to the setting out of rules. Altogether there are 47 lectures, and the last 12 of these contain descriptions of what the various genres should consist of. Historical writing, philosophical writing, fictitious history, epic and lyric poetry and dramatic poetry – all these he studies with their various subdivisions. He also provides the reader with a historical account of each genre, always having plenty to say on the comparison between Ancients and Moderns and also offering his comments on the relative value of modern European works. This is especially evident in his treatment of "fictitious history", epic poetry, tragedy and comedy.

Although he judges the efforts of different nations according to certain precepts, he makes allowance for the peculiarities of each people. Comparisons between modern works tend to be restricted to English and French literature, but he also considers Italian authors (especially in regard to epic poetry) and Spaniards. Interestingly enough, the only Italian author whom he mentions in connection with tragedy is Metastasio. In the seventh collection of the *Humanitätsbriefe* Herder also singles out Metastasio for praise.[1] Blair gives considerable attention to individual authors, particularly to those who wrote epic poems, amongst whom he includes Fénelon even though *Télémaque* is written in prose rather

[1] Herder, xviii, p. 50ff.

than verse. The observations are usually descriptive and judicial, and as far as comparative criticism is concerned they go beyond anything which has previously been discussed in this chapter. The sections dealing with the epic bear some resemblance to Voltaire's *Essay on Epick Poetry*, but Blair has a wider range of authors, and he considers all the other genres.

Another *Essay on Epic Poetry* appeared in 1782; this one, written by William Hayley, is in verse and is divided into five epistles. It covers much the same ground as the works by Voltaire and Blair, but enters into more detail. The first and second epistles deal with the rules of epic poetry and the classical authors, and Hayley even raises the question which Herder posed himself in the *Humanitätsbriefe*. Why did the Greeks have no successor to Homer? Yet he is not prepared to give an answer to this question because he believes that such problems do not lend themselves to rational analysis.

> In vain would Reason those nice questions solve,
> Which the fine play of mental powers involve.[1]

The third epistle contains a short account of Provençal literature and an evaluation of Italian, Spanish, Portuguese, French and English epic poetry. The actual text is both critical and descriptive, but Hayley also provides lengthy notes which contain much information about the various authors. Some of this is merely biographical, but there are also many descriptions of epic works. Indeed, if Hayley considers that some work is not sufficiently well known by the English public his account of it includes large extracts in translation. Thus some twenty pages are given to a description of Ercilla's *Araucana*, and in order that the English reader may become better acquainted with Camoens he is offered several sonnets.

There is nothing startling about the opinions which Hayley expresses. In spite of the fact that he has certain set requirements for an epic, which are discussed in the first and fourth epistles, he generally appears to believe in the idea of relativity. In the fifth epistle he directly attacks "the Critic's code"[2] and suggests as an alternative:

[1] William Hayley, *An Essay on Epic Poetry* (London, 1782), p. 13.
[2] *Ibid.*, p. 108.

Far wiser those, who with a generous joy,
Nor blindly fond, nor petulantly coy,
Follow each movement of the varying Muse,
Whatever step her airy form may chuse...[1]

Hayley apparently believes that every nation should have its own great epic poem and expresses the hope that his friend William Mason will furnish the British people with the epic they deserve.

James Beattie's *Dissertations Moral and Critical* (1783) brings further evidence of British interest in the literature of other nations. The section entitled *On Fable and Romance*, the only one which interests us here, contains observations about the novel in Europe which do not differ much from Blair's remarks about fictitious history. In fact he and Blair discuss almost all the same authors and their opinions about them often coincide. Beattie, however, approaches the subject from a historical point of view and provides a great deal of background information about the origin of the modern novel. Indeed, the historical portion considerably outweighs the critical portion and in spite of favourable comments about many novelists Beattie appears to have remained quite unconvinced of the value of such literature. In the concluding paragraph he says: "Let not the usefulness of Romance-writing be estimated by the length of my discourse upon it. Romances are a dangerous recreation"[2]

We have already noted that the question of the influence of Blair, Hayley and Beattie on Herder is less certain than was the case with earlier authors. It is still quite possible that Herder knew these works before he wrote any of the *Humanitätsbriefe* and he may have been indebted to them for certain factual information. Certainly he was familiar with some of the earlier writings of Blair and Beattie and respected both men. In 1767 he had praised Blair's essay on Ossian[3] and in 1772 he wrote a review of Beattie's *Essay on the Nature and Immutability of Truth*. His opinion of Beattie's work was also most favourable and he wrote about him in glowing terms. "*Beattie* ist ein Freund, ein Streiter, ein Eiferer

---

[1] *Ibid.*
[2] James Beattie, *Dissertations Moral and Critical*, 2 vols. (Dublin, 1783), II, p. 320.
[3] Herder, II, p. 161.

für die Wahrheit."[1] It is not unreasonable to suppose that he maintained an interest in the work of such men.

In this chapter we have seen how the idea of relativity gained ground in England at an early date and continued to grow during the seventeenth and eighteenth centuries. At the same time opposition to neo-classical rules or any other rules was vigorously and quite frequently voiced. Historical criticism really became established with Blackwell's work and rose to a dominant position about the middle of the eighteenth century. Together with this historical approach came a considerable increase of interest in the literature of other European nations. The writers in whose works these developments and tendencies reach their clearest expression are Addison, Blackwell, Young, the Warton brothers, Hurd, Blair and Beattie. Herder knew the work of these men, and with the possible exception of the last two they doubtless did much to stimulate his interest in and ideas about comparative literature.

[1] *Ibid.*, v, p. 456.

CHAPTER IV

THE GERMAN CRITICS

Long before the end of the seventeenth century Martin Opitz was already regarded as the founding father of modern German literature. In his *Unterricht von der Teutschen Sprache und Poesie*, published in 1682, Daniel Georg Morhof divides the history of German literature into three periods, the third of which begins with Opitz.[1] Indeed, the Germans have, or imagine they have, clearer boundary lines than either the French or the English, in critical as well as creative writing. Sigmund von Lempicki, in the only work devoted exclusively to the history of German literary criticism, studies carefully the role of Opitz.[2] Speaking of literary history he says: "Opitz geht auch hier voran."[3] and of the *Buch der Deutschen Poeterey* (1624) he states;

> Was Opitz hier aus Poetiken, philologischen Kommentaren und polyhistorischen Sammelwerken zusammenstellt, ist, – mag es noch so unbedeutend und unselbständig sein – der erste Schritt auf dem Wege zu den Tiefen der Urdichtkunst, die erst Herders helles Genie beleuchtet hat.[4]

Certainly it was no more than a first step and Opitz was prepared to admit that most of the material in the *Buch* was not new. His purpose in writing was similar to that of Du Bellay in his defence of the French

[1] Daniel Georg Morhof, *Unterricht von der Teutschen Sprache und Poesie, deren Uhrsprung, Fortgang und Lehrsätzen* (Kiel, 1682), p. 420.
[2] Sigmund von Lempicki, *Geschichte der deutschen Literaturwissenschaft bis zum Ende des 18 Jahrhunderts* (Göttingen, 1920).
[3] *Ibid.*, p. 130.　　　　[4] *Ibid.*, p. 131.

65

language. In the first paragraph of the *Buch von der Deutschen Poeterey* he acknowledges the fact that one cannot make a man into a poet by obliging him to follow certain rules. He merely wishes to offer helpful guidance to any poets who may choose to write in the German language. And, like Du Bellay, Opitz defends the use of his native language for poetry and asserts its equality with any other language. Once again we can see how a rather self-conscious nationalism leads to a relativistic point of view. The beginning of the fourth chapter has a familiar ring:

> Von dieser Deutschen Poeterey nun zue reden, sollen wir nicht vermeinen, das unser Land unter so einer rawen und ungeschlachten Lufft liege, das es nicht eben dergleichen zue der Poesie tüchtige *ingenia* könne tragen, als iergendt ein anderer ort unter der Sonnen. Wein und früchte pfleget man zue Loben von dem orte da sie herkommen sein; nicht die gemüter der menschen.[1]

Opitz does not, however, limit himself to a purely theoretic argument: he brings forward two pieces of historical evidence to prove his point. The first of these, the claim that Tacitus found a certain poetical disposition in the German people, is not particularly impressive. The second exhibit is more concrete. He mentions the flourishing period of Middle High German poetry and quotes a poem by Walther von der Vogelweide.[2] Opitz cannot explain why these early poets should have been forgotten; the best he can do is to state that modern Italian poetry only begins with Petrarch and French poetry with Ronsard,[3] thus demonstrating that early Italian and French works had also been neglected. Observations about literature in other European countries are, however, limited in the following chapters. A few passages from Ronsard's works are used to illustrate certain points, but when Opitz feels the need to go beyond German literature to demonstrate his point he generally turns to the classical models.

The earliest example in the German-speaking world of an interest in the more recent literature of other European nations appears to be contained in the work of the Swiss scholar Vadianus from St. Gallen.

[1] Martin Opitz, *Buch von der Deutschen Poeterey*, ed. R. Alewyn (Tübingen, 1963), p. 14.
[2] *Ibid.*, p. 16.
[3] Herder refers to Opitz as "der deutsche Petrarch", v, p. 372.

In his *De Poetica* (1518) he devotes one section to praise of foreign writers, especially of Dante and his contemporaries; the works which he refers to are mostly written in Latin, although he does enter a strong plea for the validity of the various European languages for literary purposes, a plea which precedes the similar one by Du Bellay by some thirty years.

The first serious study in the German language of modern European literature, as opposed to the various compendious works of sundry polyhistors is, however, contained in Morhof's *Unterricht von der Teutschen Sprache und Poesie*. Although he has received scant attention in modern times Morhof was highly regarded by his contemporaries in the latter half of the seventeenth century, including Leibniz. As Fritz Ernst puts it; "Morhof verfasste u.a. ein öfter aufgelegtes Werk, durch welches er der erste systematische Literarhistoriker Deutschlands und eine Art Vater des Komparatismus wurde."[1] Lempicki also bestows great praise upon Morhof and deals with this work in considerable detail. He says of it: "Morhofs *Unterricht* ist auf dem Gebiete der deutschen Literaturforschung des 17. Jahrhunderts unzweifelhaft die wichtigste und bedeutendste Erscheinung."[2] "Das was Morhof hier leistet-diese Geschichte der Poesie romanischer und germanischer Völker ist die erste Ahnung jenes Begriffs der modernen, romantischen Poesie, den zuerst Herder ganz allgemein gefasst hat und die Romantiker nachher ausgeführt haben."[3] This reference to Herder is not accidental, since Lempicki believes that Herder knew and studied Morhof's work. Indeed, he claims that "Herder aus diesem Buche die Rudimenta der Literaturgeschichte gelernt hat und von gewissen leitenden Gesichtspunkten dieses Buches mehr beeinflusst wurde, als man annehmen möchte."[4] Unfortunately he does not offer any evidence for this statement and there are few references to Morhof in Herder's works. In the *Alte Volkslieder* Herder refers to a poem which Morhof included in the collection of poetry published together with the *Unterricht*, but nowhere does he mention the main body of that work.

Whatever its influence on Herder, Morhof's work is clearly of great

---

[1] Fritz Ernst, *Die Schweiz als geistige Mittlerin* (Zürich, 1932), p. 16.
[2] Lempicki, *op. cit.*, p. 166.
[3] *Ibid.*, pp. 167-8.   [4] *Ibid.*, p. 171.

significance for the development of comparative literature in Germany. It is dïvided into three main parts; the first a sort of historical grammar of the German language, including some comparisons with other modern European languages, the second a historical survey of German literature which really turns into a general history of poetry and the third a sort of handbook for German poets with examples drawn from several other languages. The second and third parts are the only ones which concern us here. The second part begins with a chapter on the history of French literature and Morhof straightaway establishes the connection between the special features of language and those of literature. Each succeeding chapter contains a section dealing with the language of the nation under consideration. Morhof attaches great importance to the role of the Provençal poets, whom he believes to be the true source of most French, and indeed much Italian poetry. Of the French themselves he says: "…aber es ist gegen der *Provincialium* Poesey die ihre nichts zu schätzen, welche mehrentheils das beste auss den Provincialibus heraussgenommen."[1] He then proceeds to give an account of "la gaye science", deriving his information from Claude Fauchet, Nostradamus and Pierre de Caseneuve. In fact Morhof provides more material about Provençal poetry than any of the French or English critics we have discussed, with the exception of La Curne de Sainte-Palaye. Amongst the later French poets Marot and Ronsard are singled out for praise, whilst others, including Du Bellay and Pasquier, are merely mentioned in passing. Yet Morhof offers more than pleasant generalities and he can sometimes be quite specific in his criticism. For instance he has some reservations about Ronsard's poetry: "Er ist von hohen Einfällen, die er aber selbst bissweilen verstellet indem er gar zu viel Gelehrtheit erweisen wil."[2]

After speaking of the posthumous fame of Malherbe and giving an analysis of Voiture's odes he turns to French drama. As far as comedy is concerned attention is quite naturally focused upon Molière. Morhof displays a slight bias when he explains how Molière excelled in comedy in spite of breaking Aristotle's rules. The *Querelle des Anciens et des Modernes* had not yet broken out into the open in France, but already

---

[1] Morhof, *op. cit.*, p. 160.   [2] *Ibid.*, p. 167.

Morhof was adopting a position similar to that of such stalwart defenders of the *Anciens* as Rapin, whose work he frequently cites. Morhof's remarks about French tragedy illustrate this tendency even more clearly. "In Tragoedien hat man den Corneille und andere gehabt, welche ihr Werck woll gethan: aber es ist nicht die Krafft der Wörter und der Aussbildungen, welche bey den Griechen ist."[1] He concludes the chapter on French literature with a general appraisal, taking into account certain national characteristics. The main fault of the Frenchmen is that they are "überflüssig in der Rede" – "...welche natürliche Eygenschafft sie zu hohen tiefsinnigen Wercken ungeschickt macht."[2] Morhof supports this opinion by quoting Rapin.

The second chapter, which deals with Italian literature, opens with some observations about the relative merits of the Italian language for use in literary works. There follows a brief account of Dante, Petrarch and Boccaccio, their critics and defenders. Morhof gives further evidence in this chapter of his belief in the importance of environmental factors for the production of literature. "Die Zeit von 1400 biss 1500 hat nicht viel sonderliches hervorgebracht, weiln Krieg, Pest und allerhand Unruhe die guten Geister schier ersticket."[3] As in the previous chapter Morhof does not shrink from expressing his own opinion. He prefers Bembi to Boccaccio and Casa to Bembi. Both Ariosto and Tasso are praised, with certain reservations, but he definitely rates the latter above the former. Ariosto is, no doubt, a great writer; "seine aussbildung ist verwunderlich, seine Beschreibungen sein Meisterstücke, aber das Systema des Wercks an ihm selbsten hat nicht Vollkommenheit, die es haben soll."[4] Morhof also makes some critical remarks about Tasso, but he still concludes that Tasso is the greatest of modern Italian authors. "Solche kleine Fehler, welche die Academie della Crusca auch gross gemacht, werden leicht durch die andre Vortreflichkeiten überwogen."[5] Finally he criticizes Marino for the lack of restraint in his style.

Once again Morhof takes into account national traits when he comes to the study of Spanish literature in the third chapter. "Ich wende mich

---

[1] Morhof, *op. cit.*, p. 172. [2] *Ibid.*, p. 174.
[3] *Ibid.*, p. 194. [4] *Ibid.*, pp. 197–8.
[5] *Ibid.*, p. 204.

zu den Spaniern, einem Volcke, dessen Ernsthafftigkeit kaum der Poetischen Zierligkeit fähig zu seyn scheinen solte."[1] In spite of this he finds that the necessary spark is present in individual authors. Basing his argument on Daniel Huet's *Traité sur l'origine des romans* (1670) Morhof rejects the Spaniards' claim to be the originators of the modern novel. He firmly grants that honour to the *Provinciales*. Likewise he does not allow the contention that the French theatre owed much to Spain. The next section contains some criticism of certain national faults as seen in the works of Quevedo and Gongora.

> Es ist aber ihr Trieb zu der Tichterey mit vielen aussspürigen *Romainschen* Gedancken, als wie mit einer Kranckheit eingenommen, welche sie in allen ihren Vornehmen nothwendig Liebhaber sein. Ihre Heroische *Poemata*, ihre *Tragoedien* sein mehrentheils mit solchen Thorheiten verdorben. Sie ergiessen sich in weitläufftige *Digressiones* wie Diego Ximenes in der Eroberung von Valencia. Sie ergötzen sich in ihren Einfällen und hangen ihnen nach, wollen dinge mit weit geholten Zierrathen mehr und mehr ausssputzen.[2]

It is interesting to note the use of the word Romainsch to describe all these features, since Morhof also uses Romain to denote a novel. As Lempicki points out; "– hier wohl die erste Andeutung des Wortes romantisch, das dann auch bekanntlich mit Roman in Verbindung gesetzt wurde."[3] Since he is aware of this sligthly ridiculous aspect of Spanish literature Morhof appreciates all the more Cervantes' satire in *Don Quixote*. He considers that work to be "die artigste Satyre die jemahls gemacht werden kan."[4] He concludes the chapter with some observations about Spanish comedies, providing many details about the work of Lope de Vega.

The next chapter, which is devoted to the study of English literature, is less objective than those which precede and follow it. Evidently Morhof had recently read Rymer's introduction to his translation of Rapin, which, as we have seen, is a thoroughly nationalistic piece of work, with some unkind remarks about German language and literature. Morhof does not give the impression that he is writing *sine ira et studio*.

---

[1] *Ibid.*, p. 212.

[2] *Ibid.*, p. 216.

[3] Lempicki, *op. cit.*, p. 154.

[4] Morhof, *op. cit.*, p. 218.

To begin with, he stresses the close relationship between the English and the German language: the main difference stems from the English habit of adopting from other languages whatever can be fitted into the English language. "Wodurch sie bissweilen diesen Vorthel haben, dass sie etwas kürtzer und nachdenklicher geben können, insonderheit in Carmine."[1] Nevertheless Morhof strongly objects to Rymer's remarks about the superiority of the English language, which he considers in many respects inferior to Italian, Spanish and French. One need not look far for the cause of this adverse judgement of Rymer. "Dass er von der Teutschen (Sprache), darin so viel herrliche Poemata geschrieben so liederlich urtheilet, ist eine unverschämte Verwegenheit."[2] Morhof accuses Rymer of not knowing a word of German and goes on to assert that German is the language best suited to heroic epics, whereas the English language is dismissed as "weibisch". Furthermore English poetry is generally "zimlich verkrochen und tunckel."[3]

Nothwithstanding his strong antipathy towards Rymer, Morhof evidently relies upon him for much information in the ensuing survey of English literature. He bestows qualified praise upon Cowley and John Donne, but he shows himself unsympathetic towards Dryden because of the *Essay on Dramatic Poesy*. Again Morhof is much hurt by the haughty attitude towards the Germans. "Ich hoffe ob Gott will noch einmahl die Gelegenheit zu haben, nicht allein ihnen sondern auch andern Nationen, die dergleichen Schnarchereyen über die Teutsche machen, in einem absonderlichem Werck zu zeigen."[4] Summing up the English he admits that they have some fine works to offer, but he complains that English critics, unlike Rapin, are too nationalistic and should call themselves Panegyristas. Ben Jonson and Milton receive fleeting attention and more or less as an afterthought Morhof confesses that he has not read any of the works of Shakespeare, Fletcher or Beaumont.

The fifth chapter, which treats of Dutch literature, follows the same pattern as that of previous chapters. Moving from a discussion about the language Morhof starts his historical survey in the seventeenth century. He considers that Dutch poetry really begins in that period and owes

[1] *Ibid.*, p. 229.
[3] *Ibid.*, p. 232.
[2] *Ibid.*, p. 230.
[4] *Ibid.*, p. 248.

much to Italian and French literature. He is generous in his praise for various poets, foremost amongst whom are Jacob Catz, Constantin Huigens and Daniel Heinsius, "dessen von P. Scriverio herauss gegebene Niederländische Getichte so lieblich, süss und fliessend sein, dass ihnen nichts kan verglichen werden."[1] The opinion that "Die Schauspiele sind bey ihnen zue Vollkommenheit gebracht"[2] is somewhat surprising. Much of the credit for this is given to Jost van Vondel and Jan de Voss. At the end of the chapter Morhof summarizes his views about all of the foreign poets and critics. The essential part of these comments is contained in two sentences. "Die Meisten sprechen ihren Landsleuten zu gefallen, und urtheilen nach ihrer Zuneigung" and "Es gehet hierin nach dem gemeinen Sprichwort, dass man seinen eignen Rauch höher halte, als ein frembdes Feur."[3]

In the remainder of the second part of the *Unterricht* Morhof demonstrates that German critics are no less prone to this fault than those of any other nation. In the second of the three chapters in which he describes the development of German literature he denies that the Germans got their "Reime und die Poetische Spiele" from France. He claims that Provençal poetry only dates from 1155, that is to say in the great period of Friedrich Barbarossa and long after Otfried. He therefore concludes that the French learned much of the art of poetry from the Germans. Between the second and third periods of German literature Morhof inserts an interesting and original chapter on Nordic poetry. He attempts to discredit any claims that works from the north are older than anything which Germany has to offer. The same chauvinistic tendency is evident at the beginning of the third part of the *Unterricht*, where he defends the qualities of the German language for poetical purposes. "Vermeine also dass eine Sprache die durch die Natur und Kunst zugleich zue Vollenkommenheit gebracht, wie unsre Teutsche ist, billig vor allen andern wehrt zu halten sey."[4]

The third part contains several chapters on prosody and on literary genres, and there is plenty of discussion about the works of various foreign authors in each chapter. For instance, in the sections where he

---

[1] Morhof, *op. cit.*, pp. 261-2.
[2] *Ibid.*, pp. 264-5.
[3] *Ibid.*, pp. 274-5.
[4] *Ibid.*, pp. 464-5.

examines matters pertaining to rhyme Morhof plainly states that he does not approve of unrhymed verse. Nevertheless he describes the attitude towards this question prevalent in other countries; nor does he fail to mention some excellent works in unrhymed verse by Ariosto, Tasso, Petrarch, Milton and Abraham Mylius. He deals with many aspects of rhyme, including the origins of certain forms, and the peculiarities of each language. We find a further hint of a relativistic attitude on Morhof's part in the thirteenth chapter, where he is mainly concerned with imagery. He declares that things which are perfectly natural in one language may be totally unsuitable for another. "In allen Dingen muss Maasse gehalten werden. Man muss allezeit auff den Gebrauch und die Eigenschafft der Sprachen sehen."[1] He enters into some detail in these matters and examines the nature of metaphors quite closely. For example he claims: "Was die Teutsche Sprache anlanget, so ist sie zwar bequem genug alle Metaphoras ausszudrücken, nur in diesem reichet sie nicht zu, dass sie die Metaphorischen Epitheta so nicht geben kan, wie die Griechen, Lateiner und die heutigen Italiäner."[2] He then proceeds to elaborate upon the exact nature of German and Italian adjectives.

The same sort of penetrating analysis continues in the following chapter – *Von den Helden-Getichten*. Tasso is deemed to be the best epic poet amongst modern writers, and a general advantage in this field is conceded to the Italians. Morhof believes that the French and German languages are not suitable for epic poetry and offers a rather unexpected explanation. "Die in Teutscher wie auch in der Frantzösischen Sprache gebräuchliche art in *plurali* anzureden muss hierin gantz vermieden werden."[3] He rounds off this chapter with some observations about the novel in several different countries, claiming that the Spanish and the Italian novel were derived from the Provençal poets and not from the Arabs.

Considerable attention has been given to Morhof's *Unterricht* for several reasons. This work rises conspicuously above any others produced in the fifty years which preceded or followed it. Even if Lempicki had not assured us that Herder was familiar with it we could reasonably

[1] Morhof, *op. cit.*, p. 665.   [2] *Ibid.*, p. 667.
[3] *Ibid.*, p. 690.

suppose that he had read it. Many of the subjects which fascinated Morhof (Nordic poetry, the origins and development of the novel, the influence of Provençal poetry, the intricate connection between language and literature, to name a few of them) were of equal interest to Herder. Few other writers concerned themselves with these matters between 1682 and the publication of the first collection of *Fragmente* in 1767. Indeed, the contributions of other German writers to the development of comparative literature in this period may appear rather meagre when placed beside Morhof's effort.

This does not mean, however, that one can simply ignore the work of Hofmann von Hofmannswaldau, especially the introduction to his *Deutsche Übersetzungen und Gedichte*, which was actually published in 1679, three years before Morhof's *Unterricht*. In a few pages Hofmannswaldau does what Morhof did at much greater length in the second part of his work. He gives a historical survey of poetry, beginning with the Bible and Greek poetry and emphasizing the close links between poetry and religion. He believes "dass die ersten Glaubens-Regeln in Poesie seyn vorgetragen worden"[1] and he supports this idea by citing the example of folksongs from the Lapplanders and Indians, but he does not pursue this matter in any detail. He is definitely interested in the origins of poetry and rhyme and he concludes that the discovery of rhyme must be attributed to the Hebrews and Arabs. In Europe the Italians have apparently contributed more than any other nation to the development of poetry. Similar ideas were expressed in France and England by Pasquier and Rymer.

> Da ich denn bekenne, dass kein Volck in Europa so zeitlich die Poesie zur Annehmlichkeit und in Ansehen bracht, als eben die Welschen, so solche an der Provenzalischen Reimens-Art, da sie lange einheimisch gewesen, hervorgezogen, und wegen Reinlichkeit der Sprache dergestalt verbessert, dass auch solche nachmahls allzeit auf einerley Art, durch mehr als 300 Jahr ungeändert verblieben ist.[2]

Pride of place is handed to Petrarch, who served as a "Richtschnur" to

[1] Christian Hofmann von Hofmannswaldau, *Deutsche Übersetzungen und Gedichte* (Breslau, 1710), p. 5.
[2] *Ibid.*, pp. 7-8.

74

all the poets who followed him. Hofmannswaldau mentions specifically Ariosto, Tasso, Marino, Caporali, Fulvio, Testi, Achilini and Gratiani. He claims that French peotry did not really begin to develop until the period of François I, when the French language began "sich ziemlich zu verbessern." He appears to adopt a somewhat prejudiced and unhistorical attitude when he mentions the work of various early French poets and adds the comment, "so ist doch wegen der unartigen Sprache alles dergestalt hart und unannehmlich, dass itzige verwehnte Ohren es nicht ohne Verdruss vertragen können."[1] Amongst the later French poets he particularly admires Melin, Marot, Ronsard and Malherbe and he gives favourable mention to Geodau, Du Bellay, Le Moyne, Chapelain, Scudéry and the Corneille brothers. He does not enter into any detailed criticism, except in the case of Ronsard, whom he blames for relying too much upon classical authors.

Hofmannswaldau reckons that Spanish was even slower in developing into a poetic language. He sees the beginning of Spanish poetry in the works of Boscan and Garcilaso about one hundred and seventy years before the time when he was writing. "...und ist vor ihnen keine richtig abgefasste Poesie, oder eintziges Sonnet zu sehen gewesen."[2] The same bias against older works of literature is evident in his remarks about English, Dutch and German poetry. Chaucer is rated below Spenser, Michael Drayton, Jonson, Quarles and Donne because he lacks their "Gelehrigkeit, Kunst und Lieblichkeit."[3] Dutch poetry begins with Heinsius and Hofmannswaldau has little patience with the Old High German language and "Otfrieds unverständliche Reimen". He even provides an example of the latter's verse in order to show how poor it is. He does, however, show some appreciation for the Middle High German poets, quoting passages from Wolfram von Eschenbach and Walther von der Vogelweide. He brings the history of German poetry up to his own time, paying due homage to Opitz. His conclusion from this examination of German and foreign poetry does not come as a surprise: "Diss werde ich mich noch beyzufügen unterstehen, dass durch gedachter Männer Fleiss und Nachsinnen, die Teutsche Poesie so reine worden, dass

[1] *Ibid.*, p. 9.   [2] *Ibid.*, p. 11.
[3] *Ibid.*

sie der Ausländischen nichts mehr nachgiebet."[1] We have already seen how Morhof found all critics to be biased in favour of their own country. In the following section of the introduction Hofmannswaldau appears to shake himself free from this fault when he says:

> Dieses gestehe ich gerne, dass die Welschen, wegen ihrer ingemein angebohrnen Verstandes und Scharffsinnigkeit, an guter Erfindung (wiewohl auch bey allen nicht alles von gleicher Güte) den Teutschen manchesmal zuvor gehen.[2]

Yet he hastens to qualify such an admission and criticizes the Italians for their excessive use of abbreviations in poetry. Although this work is of modest scope, Hofmannswaldau deserves credit for the interest which he showed in the poetry of other European nations at a time when such interest was quite uncommon.

When examining Morhof's *Unterricht* we noted how he took exception to disparaging remarks about German language and literature. In this he was not alone. Père Bouhours' notorious comment about the primitive state of the Germans and the impossibility of their achieving any higher level of culture provoked other writers. In 1708 Barthold Feind published a collection of poetry – *Deutsche Gedichte* – with a lengthy preface entitled *Von dem Temperament und Gemühts-Beschaffenheit eines Poeten und Gedancken von der Opera*. Feind attempts to discover the ideal natural temperament for a poet, and initially leads us to hope for a comparative survey of poetry. "Weil ich mich aber an der Frantzosen Rodomontaden nicht gross kehre als welche gewohnet sind nichts für gut zu erkennen was nicht auf ihrem Mist gewachsen, so will ich sehen wie die Teutsche denen Ausländern nachgeahmet."[3] Unfortunately he does not provide much solid material and reaches few conclusions about the poetic temperament. He does, however, foreshadow, albeit for quite different reasons, an important shift of interest from French to English literature which took place towards the middle of the century with the help of Lessing and others. Feind finds many reasons for rejecting French tragedy, principal of which is the lack of action. In this

---

[1] Hofmannswaldau, *op. cit.*, p. 25.　　　　[2] *Ibid.*
[3] Barthold Feind, *Deutsche Gedichte* (Stade, 1708), p. 40.

connection he cites the example of the English in contrast and even mentions the fact, "dass etliche, wenn sie des renommirten Englischen Tragici Shakespeare Trauer-Spiele verlesen hören, offt lautes Halses an zu schreyen gefangen und häuffige Thränen vergossen."[1] Unfortunately Feind provides no further details and so this work can scarcely be called the start of Shakespearean criticism in Germany.

The nationalistic tone which pervades Feind's introduction to the *Deutsche Gedichte* is also evident in many other critical works during the first half of the eighteenth century. Occasionally this would lead, as we have already observed ln the case of several French and English critics, to support for the idea of relativity. This point is nicely illustrated in a work by J. G. Meister which otherwise has little to offer in the way of comparative literature. On the first page of his *Unvorgreiffliche Gedancken von Teutschen Epigrammatibus* (1726) Meister asserts: "Denn eine iegliche Nation scheinet ihr besondernes Naturel, ein iegliches Jahrhundert seinen Genium, und ein ieglich Alter seine Zuneigung zu haben." He goes on to reject the French distinction between 'bon esprit' and 'bel esprit' (the Germans had been consigned to the former category, thereby automatically ruling out the possibility of great original writing) and claims that the Germans have no less bright a future just because they are late in achieving a high level of culture.

Gottlieb Stolle is also hopeful about the future of German poetry in his *Anleitung zur Historie der Gelahrtheit* (1718). The fifth chapter of the first part consists of a general history of poetry. Drawing his information from Crescimbeni, Rapin and Baillet he gives a brief appraisal of the heroic poetry of Tasso, Ariosto, Chapelain, Desmarets de Saint-Sorlin, LeMoyne and Scudéry. He also relies upon the French critics for his judgement of Corneille, Racine and Molière; and since he was unable to glean much from those sources he has little to say about English or Spanish literature.

Stolle's particular importance lies in the fact that he introduced into Germany the quarrel between the *Anciens* and the *Modernes*. Instead of using the nationalistic approach of Meister he sided with the *Modernes*

---

[1] *Ibid.*, p. 109.

and used some of the arguments put forward by Perrault. It is interesting to note how strongly Stolle objects to the dominance of classical authors over German writing, some twelve years before the publication of Gottsched's *Versuch einer critischen Dichtkunst*. He recommends that German poets stick to their own language and despises poetical handbooks. "Denn wer zum Poeten gebohren ist, bedarff dergleichen Bücher eben so wenig, als Virgilus, Ovidius, Opitz, Hoffmannswaldau und andre rechtschaffne Tichter."[1] Yet Stolle lacks any historical feeling; not only does he repeat some of Perrault's arguments against Homer, he even criticizes Ronsard in the following manner: "Und wie sich die Sprache seit der Zeit sehr geändert und man den numerum poeticum und die delicatesse besser studiret, so kan er freylich nicht mehr einer der besten Tichter heissen."[2] There is no evidence that Herder read Stolle's work, but Stolle does seem to have anticipated some of the arguments which were to be used against neo-classicism in Germany.

And now let us turn to J. C. Gottsched and the establishment of German neo-classicism. His *Versuch einer critischen Dichtkunst* (1730) is generally accepted as the most representative work of his literary criticism and its influence lasted for many years. As Lempicki points out, even Goethe, in the seventh book of *Dichtung und Wahrheit*, had some words of praise for its historical usefulness. This is not the place to discuss all the implications of the *Dichtkunst* for German literature, and we will limit ourselves to the question of how much Gottsched took into consideration the literature of other European nations. In fact it will be seen that he was no less interested in foreign writing than those other representatives of classical conservatism, Rapin and Rymer. Certainly Gottsched was not lacking in patriotism. In his *Lob- und Gedächtnisrede auf Martin Opitz* he says: "Wenn sich nämlich unsre Deutschen auf Künste und Wissenschaften beflissen haben; so haben sie es auch gemeiniglich, aus eignem Triebe, ihren Lehrmeistern und Vorgängern weit zuvor getan."[3] Nevertheless he could not resort to the arguments of Meister and so many others; he had to turn to French literature for elucidation of the

[1] Gottlieb Stolle, *Anleitung zur Historie der Gelahrtheit* (Jena, 1727), p. 167.
[2] *Ibid.*, p. 164.
[3] J. C. Gottsched, *Gesammelte Schriften*, ed. E. Reichel, 6 vols. (Berlin, 1902), v., p. 112.

78

classical rules, and he accepted the superiority of the French in the past, whilst promising a great future for the Germans.

Gottsched was even prepared to press the claim for German superiority when considering the origins of poetry in the distant past. In the first section of the *Dichtkunst* he declares:

> Wie nun die Griechen in ihrem Sylbenmaasse die Lateiner zu Nachfolgern bekommen haben: so haben auch die alten Deutschen ganz Europa reimen gelehret. Italien, Spanien und Gallien nahmen die Art derjenigen Völker an, die sich durch die Gewalt der Waffen ihrer bemächtigten. Die Dänen, Schweden, Holl- und Engländer sind selbst von deutschem Geschlechte, und haben also die Kunst von ihren eigenen Vorfahren gefasset.[1]

The *Dichtkunst* does not contain any historical survey of literary activities in various European countries, in the manner of Morhof's *Unterricht*. When Gottsched considers all the genres and many different aspects of poetry he does, however, include some observations about modern European literature. In the second chapter, which deals with the character of a poet, he insists upon the necessity of a sound knowledge of human behaviour. This may sound extremely jejune, but the point that he is really trying to make is that a poet should imitate human actions. In contrast to this he cites the example of Tasso and Milton; "Denn wenn gleich einige, wie Tasso, Milton, und seine Nachahmer unter uns, auch Engeln und Teufel nachzuahmen gesuchet: so ist dieses so zu reden, aus ihrer Sphäre ausgeschweifet."[2] In the chapter entitled *Von dem Wunderbaren in der Poesie* he returns to this theme and this time includes Voltaire's *Henriade* in the criticism, especially since Voltaire had focused attention on exactly the same fault in Tasso and Milton in his *Essay on Epic Poetry*. In this connection he speaks most favourably of Cervantes' *Don Quixote*, a book which has helped do away with extravagant adventure stories.

Gottsched, referring to Tasso's angels and devils, almost gives the impression that he subscribes to the idea of relativity. "Es ist gewiss, dass man diese Leute mit der herrschenden Meynung ihrer abergläubischen

---

[1] J. C. Gottsched, *Versuch einer critischen Dichtkunst* (Darmstadt, 1962), pp. 76-7.
[2] *Ibid.*, p. 107.

Zeiten eben so wohl entschuldigen kann; als die alten Poeten, wegen der Fabeln von ihren Göttern, in Betrachtung der heidnischen Theologie, entschuldiget werden."[1] He immediately adds, however, that it is better "sich solcher Arten des Wunderbaren zu bedienen, die allen Zeiten und Orten gemein sind und bleiben." In fact, in the chapter *Vom guten Geschmacke eines Poeten* he addresses himself directly to this question. He recognizes that certain critics rebel at the idea of using the Athenians as a standard for all time and he even admits: "Der Einwurf scheint wichtig zu seyn."[2] His reply to this objection demonstrates how firmly he believed in the classical rules and in the ability of a rational eighteenth century man to distinguish true beauty from that which stems from ephemeral fashion.

> Diejenigen bleiben also nur an der äussersten Schale kleben, die sich einbilden, die poetischen Schönheiten wären ganz willkührlich; heute könnte diess, und morgen was anders gefallen; in Rom könnte was hässlich seyn, was in Paris oder London unvergleichlich wäre. Nicht der Beyfall macht eine Sache schön; sondern die wahre Schönheit erwirbt sich bey allen Verständigen den Beyfall.[3]

This passage also serves to illustrate the point that an interest in comparative literature is not the prerogative of any single school of thought, ancient or modern, classical or relativistic. Gottsched and Herder held quite disparate views about literature in general, but each contributed in his own way to comparative literature. In this respect Gottsched has perhaps been treated unjustly through the years. Obviously his contribution in this field was not as great as that of Herder, either in quantity or in quality, but this does not alter the fact that he concerned himself with foreign literature at a time when few other writers in Germany had done so. In any historical survey of comparative literature he should not be passed over in silence solely because of his neo-classical opinions.

Gottsched's bias is quite evident in the chapter, *Von der Wahrscheinlichkeit in der Poesie*. According to him probability is absolutely essential in poetry and he hastens to explain exactly what he means by this. "Ich verstehe nämlich durch die poetische Wahrscheinlichkeit nichts anders,

[1] *Ibid.*, p. 182.   [2] *Ibid.*, p. 132.
[3] *Ibid.*, p. 133.

als die Ähnlichkeit des Erdichteten, mit dem, was wirklich zu geschehen pflegt; oder die Übereinstimmung der Fabel mit der Natur."[1] Working on this principle he proceeds to criticize in some detail the works of Camoens, Ercilla, Tasso, Ariosto, Marino, Milton and Voltaire, quoting passages from some of them in the original. Milton was subjected to severe criticism even before Gottsched's quarrel with the Swiss critics. In an early chapter, when making some claims for German poetry, he admits that Reinecke Fuchs, Theuerdank and Froschmäuseler and certain other works may not be the equal of Homer, Virgil and Tasso, but, he adds, "so sind sie doch nicht schlechter, als das, was Marino, Ariost, Chapelain, St. Amand und Milton in diesem Stücke geliefert haben."[2] Much of the same criticism is repeated in the chapter *Von dem Heldengedichte*. In *Vom Wohlklange der poetischen Schreibart* there is a brief analysis of the sorts of rhyme to be found in English, Italian and French poetry. Gottsched quotes with disapproval two passages, from Tasso and Addison, where three consecutive lines rhyme. He considers this as too much of a good thing. On the other hand he favours the English predilection for unrhymed verse on the stage and even admits: "In diesem Stücke haben die heutigen Engländer auch vor den Franzosen den Vorzug."[3]

In the chapter on the satirical epic Gottsched considers with a fair amount of detail the work of Tassoni, Butler, Boileau, Pope and Voltaire. In this case he appears to be more willing than usual to consider what other European writers have done and to judge them on their own merits, rather than automatically criticizing them according to classical rules. The section under the title *Von dogmatischen Gedichten* is surprisingly short, and more attention is devoted to German than to foreign writers. Indeed, Gottsched seems momentarily to turn everything upside down. Young and Boileau are each dismissed unexpectedly in one sentence. Of the former he says: "und Yong (sic) hat in seinen *Night-Thoughts*, vom Leben, Tode, und der Unsterblichkeit, auf eine sehr philosophische Art gehandelt."[4] Boileau, one of the pillars of French neo-classicism merely receives the following acknowledgement:

[1] Gottsched, *Dichtkunst*, p. 198. [2] *Ibid.*, p. 87.
[3] *Ibid.*, p. 407. [4] *Ibid.*, p. 573.

"Boileau, hat die Dichtkunst, in ein ordentliches Lehrgedicht gebracht; an dessen Ordnung und Einrichtung gleichwohl ein holländisches Frauenzimmer, Jungf. Hooghard in ihren *Lettres Antipoetiques* sehr viel auszusetzen gefunden."[1] Evidence that Gottsched was not completely prejudiced against English literature, except as far as drama was concerned, is provided in the chapter dealing with pastoral poetry. After he has discussed and criticized the works of Tasso, Guarini, Marot, Ronsard and Fontenelle he turns to the English poets and declares: "Pope aber hat sie ohne Zweifel alle übertroffen."[2] Furthermore he concludes the chapter with a four-page extract from Steele's observations on the nature of pastoral poetry, since he considers this to be an unusually good treatment of the subject in spite of "die Eigenliebe der englischen Nation gegen sich selbst."[3]

In the chapter on comedy Gottsched again has some words of praise for English authors. Naturally he rates French comedy as the finest in modern Europe, and he supports this opinion with an analysis of Molière's qualities. His nationalistic tendencies come to the surface again when he claims that the Germans under the guiding hand of Charlemagne were the first people in all of Europe in the middle ages to revive enthusiasm for drama. He is more modest about German comedy of the preceding century. In spite of some severe criticism of English comedy Gottsched ranks it well above Italian comedy. He rejects the various claims about humour on the stage and the emphasis on original characters, but he agrees with St. Evremond and Voltaire, "dass die englische Komödie sehr viel moralische lasterhafte Charactere glücklich aufführet; und darinn an Reichthum und Nachdruck allen andern Nationen vorgeht."[4] Here, as in all the rest of the *Dichtkunst* Gottsched offers little information about foreign authors which was not already available in Morhof's *Unterricht*. Indeed, it appears probable that Gottsched obtained much of his material from Morhof.[5] The most important thing about the *Dichtkunst* in regard to comparative literature is the fact that Gottsched expresses an opinion about many works from other

[1] *Ibid.* [2] *Ibid.*, p. 590.
[3] *Ibid.*, p. 591. [4] *Ibid.*, p. 640.
[5] Gottsched cites Morhof's *Unterricht* on several occasions. *Versuch*, pp. 70, 83, 456, 793.

European nations. He did not provide much new information and his opinions may have already appeared outmoded to Herder, but his interest in the literary activities of neighbouring countries was a definite step along the road towards comparative literature.

Although Gottsched's ideas held sway in Germany during much of the first half of the eighteenth century, by the time of his death in 1766 he was a generally discredited figure on the literary scene. Such a complete reversal of fortune came largely as a result of his protracted quarrel with the critics of Zürich, J. J. Bodmer and J. J. Breitinger. The substance of the feud, especially the aesthetic questions, does not concern us here: it has been amply documented and an account of it may be found in any of the standard histories of German literature. Suffice it to say that Bodmer and Breitinger have generally been regarded as the progressive force. As Saintsbury puts it; "There can, however, be no reasonable question that the pair were – more than any other pair or person – responsible for the Rally of Germany."[1] It is difficult to take these writers separately, since they collaborated on so many of their works, and in many cases, e.g. Breitinger's *Kritische Dichtkunst* (1740), it is almost impossible to tell who wrote any particular section.[2]

Authorship is, however, much clearer in regard to comparative literature than to theoretical writings. Although one cannot name any single work comparable to Morhof's *Unterricht* there is no doubt, if one looks at his career as a whole, that Bodmer was a practitioner of comparative literature. Together with Breitinger he introduced the form of the *Spectator* essay into German literature and on his own he translated Milton's *Paradise Lost*, Homer, some old English ballads, *Hudibras* and the *Dunciad*. In addition he generally followed a historical approach towards criticism and discovered some of the great monuments of German mediaeval literature, including *Parzival*, the *Nibelungenlied*, and

---

[1] Saintsbury, *op. cit.*, III, p. 21.

[2] Saintsbury said of their works: "All these might, with advantage, be more accessible than they are. The originals appear to be rare, and when they occur are dear, and at once carried off." (III, p. 24n.) The situation has only begun to improve quite recently as the J. B. Metzlersche Verlagsbuchhandlung of Stuttgart has produced facsimile editions of several of their works.

many works of the Minnesänger. He was also the first critic to defend Dante in Germany with historical arguments. As Wellek says of him: "He represents a new taste and, in Germany, the first lively feeling for history."[1] This historical awareness is particularly evident in his *Critische Betrachtungen uber die poetischen Gemählde der Dichter* (1741). It contains two chapters which explain how each nation has its own character and "Redensart". Bodmer declares that it is necessary for any good translator to undergo a sort of "Einfühlen": in this respect he mentions how he would like to defend Homer against some of the inept and unhistorical criticism which was aimed at him. We have no proof that Bodmer was familiar with Blackwell's work at this time, but he seems to have had a similar idea of historical criticism,[2] and a connection appears quite likely.

Bodmer reveals this same historical awareness in the section where he examines in some detail Dante's *La Divina Commedia* and Cervantes' *Don Quixote*. Indeed, whenever he wrote about Dante he particularly stressed this point; his *Neue Critische Briefe* (1749) and several contributions to the *Freymüthigen Nachrichten* bear witness to this fact. It is interesting to note Lempicki's summary of Bodmer's activity in this field.

> Die Danteaufsätze Bodmers sind die ersten Anzeichen der historischen Literaturbetrachtung in Deutschland. Bodmer verlangt, dass man das Werk aus der Zeit, in der es entstand, und aus der Absicht seines Schöpfers zu verstehen trachte, dass man "ein originales Genie" weder an antiken Mustern messe noch nach modernen Regeln beurteile, dass man den "Mittelpunkt" des Gedichtes zu erfassen versuche und sich in den "Plan" des Dichters bestrebe hineinzudenken. Vor allem aber betont Bodmer, dass man der Individualität des Dichters Gerechtigkeit widerfahren lasse.[3]

I have quoted this passage at some length because of the striking resemblance between Bodmer's ideas and those of Herder. Apart from the

---

[1] Wellek, *A History of Modern Criticism*, I, p. 147.

[2] Max Wehrli, *J. J. Bodmer und die Geschichte der Literatur* (Leipzig, 1936), p. 81 says: "Thomas Blackwells *Inquiry into the life and writings of Homer* erschien 1735 und ist Bodmer offenbar bald bekannt geworden." Yet he offers no proof of this assertion beyond the statement: "Er benützt die Schrift mehrfach in seinen Betrachtungen über die poetischen Gemälde."

[3] Lempicki, *op. cit.*, p. 276.

first sentence it would be perfectly reasonable to substitute the name Herder for that of Bodmer. It is difficult to establish exactly how much of Bodmer's works Herder read, but in the eighth collection of the *Humanitätsbriefe* he pays him the following tribute:

> auch Bodmers Bemühungen aus neueren sowohl ausländischen, als unsrer alten Deutschen Sprache uns einen grösseren Reichthum an Gedanken, Bildern, Fabeln, Einkleidungen und Ausdrücken als Kunstrichter und Dichter zuzuführen, haben ihren Zweck nicht verfehlet. Er hat viel aufgeregt, und sich fast über Vermögen bemühet, indem er bis in sein greises Alter wie der frischeste Jüngling an jedem neuen Product unsrer Sprache Theil nahm.[1]

Breitinger's contribution to comparative literature cannot be so clearly defined as that of Bodmer, but at least he had a hand in writing *Von dem Einfluss und Gebrauche der Einbildungs-Krafft zur Ausbesserung des Geschmackes* (1727). This is one of the few works of the Swiss critics which specifically contains some comparative criticism. They move from a comparison of the German excellence in describing the "todten Wercken der Natur" with the French ability in "der scharf-sinnigen Schreibart"[2] to a comparison of Postel's *Wittekind* with the works of Tasso and Marino. Then there is a comparison between a physical description by Lohenstein and Addison, to the advantage of the latter, and the works of several German authors upon a similar theme are measured against one another. The works of Theophrastus, La Bruyère, Shaftesbury, Joachim Rachel and Opitz are also placed side by side. The final section, which is the most interesting of all for our purposes, opens with the statement that national characteristics are determined by three factors. Firstly by climate, secondly by the form of government and thirdly by education; these national traits are also assumed to show through in the literature of each country. To illustrate this point we are offered a comparison of the dramatic treatment of Queen Sophonisbe by authors from four different nations, Corneille, Trissino, Nathaniel Lee and Lohenstein. Corneille, as one might expect of a Frenchman, sticks closely to the *Anciens* and makes

[1] Herder, XVIII, p. 128.
[2] J. J. Bodmer und J. J. Breitinger, *Von dem Einfluss und Gebrauche der Einbildungs-Krafft zur Ausbesserung des Geschmackes* (Frankfurt and Leipzig, 1727), p. 21.

Sophonisbe love her city of Carthage more than any husband. Trissino makes her fear the Romans more than anything else. Lee depicts her as an extremely proud character with a deep love for Masinissa. In spite of the fact that he is the German representative Lohenstein is criticized more than any of the others. He is described as an erratic poet, "der uns seine gelehrten Sprüche und belesene Metaphorn mit unangenehmer Freygebigkeit zuwirfft."[1] There follows a similar analysis of the character of Masinissa. We have already seen how Pasquier and Rymer used the method of comparing passages of similar content from writers of different nations, but Bodmer and Breitinger were the first to use this approach in German criticism. With this chapter on the various versions of *Sophonisbe* they appear to have been the first critics anywhere to attempt to use this method on a larger scale. Like Herder, some forty years later, the Swiss critics attempted to consider literature together with its environment.

Johann Elias Schlegel has generally been considered as a member of Gottsched's circle in Leipzig, a view for which there is some justification. Certainly the dramas which he wrote do not go beyond the rules which Gottsched laid down. Nevertheless Friedrich Braitmaier denies that Schlegel was influenced by Gottsched in any significant manner. "Schlegel ist nie Gottschedianer gewesen und ausgegangen ist er, wenigstens in der ästhetischen Theorie, von den Schweizern."[2] Although this denial is perhaps slightly exaggerated it is true that some of his ideas were much closer to those of Bodmer and Breitinger than to the conservative classicism which was dominant in Leipzig. This definitely applies to his interest in English literature; both Schlegel and Bodmer did much to bring English works to the attention of the German-speaking public, not as in the case of Gottsched for the sake of censure, but rather to serve as models in many respects. Indeed, Schlegel has rightly been regarded as the forerunner of Lessing's famous seventeenth *Litteraturbrief,* since he suggested that the English dramatists had followed Aristotle's rules more truly than had their French counterparts.

[1] Bodmer und Breitinger, *op. cit.,* p. 230.
[2] Friedrich Braitmaier, *Geschichte der poetischen Theorie und Kritik,* 2 vols (Frauenfeld, 1888–9), I, p. 249.

Of course Bodmer also proclaimed the merits of English literature, but he devoted less attention than Schlegel did to the drama, and it is doubtful whether he ever read any of Shakespeare's plays.[1] Schlegel was the first real propagator of Shakespeare's works in Germany. Admittedly Schlegel's influence was not great in his own time and he died too young to have made a substantial mark in the literary world. As Gundolf puts it: "Als Tendenz ist Schlegel ein Vorläufer Lessings, mag dieser von ihm beeinflusst sein oder nicht. In beiden ist dieselbe Willensrichtung der Zeit deutlich, in dem einen schwächer und dumpfer, im anderen stärker und bewusster."[2] The first of the works dealing with Shakespeare was written in 1741, shortly after the publication of C. W. von Borck's translation of *Julius Caesar*, but it did not appear until the following year in Gottsched's *Beyträge zur critischen Historie der deutschen Sprache, Poesie und Beredsamkeit*.

According to Gundolf, Schlegel wrote his *Vergleichung Shakespears und Andreas Gryphs bey Gelegenheit einer Übersetzung Shakespears 'Julius Cäsar'* at the instigation of Gottsched, who had already assailed the translation himself and wanted Schlegel to make a thorough job of it. To be sure, Schlegel begins the piece with some detailed criticism of Borck's translation, but he aims chiefly at Borck's failure to master the German language; and it soon becomes apparent that Schlegel's attitude towards Shakespeare is altogether more tolerant than that of Gottsched, or any other critic outside England whom we have yet encountered. Voltaire was extremely erratic in his praise of the great English writer and in the final analysis turned out to be a harsh critic. Although Schlegel was also sympathetic towards the classical rules in drama, he was unstinting

---

[1] As Braitmaier points out: "Nur zweimal führt er Shakespeare als 'Sasper' an. Das einemal rühmt er nach dem Spectator seine treffliche Schilderung von Jagdhunden, das andremal die seiner 'Geister und Phantasiewesen'", I, p. 220. There has been some dispute about the form 'Sasper': some believe that Bodmer was merely changing the name to suit the Swiss dialect, others hold that he simply did not know any better. At any rate his knowledge of Shakespeare was surely meagre. Gundolf puts it in a nutshell: "Die Entdeckung Shakespeares durch die Schweizer war zunächst ein Zufall, von der durch Lessing unterschieden wie die erste Entdeckung Amerikas durch verschlagene Seefahrer vom planmässigen Zug des Kolumbus." Friedrich Gundolf, *Shakespeare und der deutsche Geist* (Berlin, 1922), p. 106.
[2] Gundolf, *op. cit.*, p. 115.

in his praise of Shakespeare's qualities. Unlike Voltaire he disposes of the irregularity of Shakespeare's works quite quickly; after stating: "Das erste, das man bey einem Schauspiele zu beobachten hat, ist die Einrichtung desselben."[1] he goes on to make some general observations about English drama compared with German drama. Basing his judgement of the latter upon Gryphius' *Leo Armenius* he shows how the plot is carefully constructed; everything hinges upon the construction of the play. As for the English, "so sind ihre Schauspiele mehr Nachahmungen der Personen, als Nachahmungen einer gewissen Handlung."[2] Instead of dwelling upon the negative aspects he proceeds to examine the strength of English drama.

Schlegel analyses the manner in which Shakespeare presents his characters, noting how one character in a play describes another and furnishing several examples of this from *Julius Caesar*. He contrasts this with Gryphius' approach to the matter and enters into a discussion of the best method of portraying historical characters on the stage. By holding closely to the historical facts Gryphius avoids the risk of offending the spectator, who may be familiar with all the traditional accounts of the character. On the other hand Shakespeare gains much by inventing his characters and thus having them more completely before him. He manages to produce "diese kühnen und doch sehr nachdrücklichen und lebhaften Züge eines Charakters"[3] to which Gryphius rarely rises. Schlegel considers that both playwrights show a tendency to be "schwülstig" and use excessively colourful imagery, the difference being that Shakespeare leaves some space between "jeglicher Gemüthsbewegung" and Gryphius does not. Likewise Shakespeare enjoys an advantage in the creation of "Sittensprüche". "Bey dem Shakespear aber scheinet überall eine noch tiefere Kenntniss der Menschen hervorzuleuchten, als bey dem Gryph. Obgleich die Sittensprüche auch bei diesem Letztern desswegen nicht gemein sind."[4] Schlegel concludes the essay with some remarks about faults which are common to both writers and recommends that the reader compare the two works himself.

[1] Johann Elias Schlegel, *Ausgewählte Werke*, ed. W. Schubert (Weimar, 1963), p. 462.
[2] *Ibid.*   [3] *Ibid.*, p. 472.
[4] *Ibid.*, p. 474.

Schlegel's last work, *Gedanken zur Aufnahme des dänischen Theaters*, was written in 1747, but was not published until 1764. This essay contains much sound advice to the Danes about the policies they should adopt in establishing a national theatre in Copenhagen. Schlegel reveals himself as a firm advocate of the idea of relativity. "Denn eine jede Nation schreibt einem Theater, das ihr gefallen soll, durch ihre verschiedenen Sitten auch verschiedene Regeln vor, und ein Stück, das für die eine Nation gemacht ist, wird selten den andern ganz gefallen."[1] This theme is reiterated throughout the work. He goes on to illustrate his argument by pointing out in considerable detail the differences between French and English literature, and he relates this to variations in national character. For instance, the French like a simple plot without any sub-plots, which moves forward in a straight line, whereas the English with their "Geschwindigkeit und Ungeduld im Denken" prefer to have all sorts of complicated and apparently unconnected sub-plots, which are all tied together at the end. One result of this is the following: "Der Engländer erwuchert dadurch viele kleine Anmerkungen über das menschliche Leben, kleine Scherze, kleine Abschilderungen der Natur, welche der Franzos nicht leichtlich auf sein Theater bringen kann."[2] The Frenchmen are unable to break the logical sequence of events.

Schlegel continues to contrast French and English habits and he leaves the impression that he prefers the English way despite his belief in the idea of relativity. He explains that the Frenchman sees love as the main occupation both in life and on the stage, whereas the Englishman manages to put it in perspective and consider other important matters. The English also pay far more attention to characterization than the French; the latter concern themselves only with the main figure of a drama, and even then they fall back on servants and confidants to explain their masters to the audience. "Man muss auch bekennen, dass in dieser Wahl und Bestimmung der Charaktere die grösste Stärke der englischen Komödie besteht; deren gute Poeten auch sogar die Grade derselben zu bestimmen wissen."[3] Nor does Schlegel restrict himself to citing Shakespeare as an example; Steele, Cibber and Congreve are mentioned here.

---

[1] Schlegel, *op. cit.*, p. 560.   [2] *Ibid.*   [3] *Ibid.*, p. 578.

The most surprising blow in favour of the English dramatists is yet to come. Schlegel pursues a line of attack which Lessing followed more than a decade later. Speaking of the classical rules and the three unities he says: "Die Wahrheit zu gestehen, beobachten die Engländer, die sich keiner Einheit des Ortes rühmen, dieselbe grossentheils viel besser, als die Franzosen, die sich damit viel wissen, dass sie die Regeln des Aristoteles so genau beobachten."[1] Schlegel points out that it is more reasonable to switch the scene from one house to another than to bring a character into his rival's house, where he would never normally appear, simply because the first part of the action has occurred there. Although Schlegel clearly supports the rules he is also well aware of the danger of overlooking the inner harmony of a drama by placing too much emphasis on outer form. The piece was written for the benefit of the Danes, but he includes the Germans in his concluding words of advice. "Die Deutschen haben den Fehler begangen, dass sie ohne Unterschied allerley Komödien aus dem Französischen übersetzt haben, ohne vorher zu überlegen, ob die Charaktere derselben auch auf ihre Sitten sich schickten."[2] This provides us with a clue as to Schlegel's motives in concerning himself with foreign literature. After his death in 1749 many other critics, including some of the most distinguished, turned their minds to similar problems and considered the development of a national German literature to compare with the achievements of other European nations. Whether Herder read the *Vergleichung* or the *Gedanken* is not certain, but he was without doubt familiar with some of Schlegel's other works. In 1767 he reviewed for the *Allgemeine Deutsche Bibliothek* the fourth volume of his collected works, published by Johann Heinrich Schlegel. Herder's opinion of his critical writings was high, although he was less enthusiastic about the original poetry. "Wer Schl. in seinen Theatralischen Stücken, in seinen Abhandlungen, und in seinen Horazischen Briefen zu schätzen weis: wird es ihm leicht verzeihen, dass er kein Odendichter, oder kein Anakreontist vom ersten Range ist."[3]

We now pass on to one of the most important German critics of the eighteenth century, Gotthold Ephraim Lessing. We have already ob-

[1] *Ibid.*, p. 582.   [2] *Ibid.*, p. 583.
[3] Herder, IV, p. 239.

90

served that many men of letters shared Schlegel's interest in the development of a worthy national German literature, and Lessing was definitely amongst their number. By his critical writings and the example of his own dramatic works he did as much as any man to bring about the great revival of German letters. In pursuing this end he also incidentally contributed to the development of comparative literature. We have already referred in passing to the seventeenth *Litteraturbrief* (1759), in which Lessing repeats with great force some of the ideas put forward by Schlegel. In the process of annihilating the Gottschedian arguments in favour of French classical drama he builds up the reputation of English drama, and especially Shakespeare. Like Schlegel he believes in the Aristotelian rules and declares that Shakespeare unwittingly observed them more satisfactorily than the French dramatists did. Lessing also considers the matter of national taste and assumes that the Germans are naturally much closer to the English than to the French.

Numerous observations about French, English and Italian literature are scattered throughout the rest of the *Litteraturbriefe*. In the nineteenth and twentieth letters he tries to explain why the hexameter did not become a popular metre in English poetry. He concludes that this is simply due to a lack of example. "Hätte *Milton* den Hexameter zu seinem *Verlornen Paradiese* gewählt, so würde er längst der Lieblingsvers der Nation geworden seyn, wenn der Dichter auch nicht das geringste zu seiner Anpreisung gesagt hätte."[1] In the sixty-third and sixty-fourth letters Lessing offers a detailed comparison of Wieland's *Lady Johanna Gray* and Nicholas Rowe's *Lady Jane Gray*. This is a fine example of Lessing in his most devastating form. To begin with he praises Wieland's play and says that it is so good that it has actually been plagiarized in England. After making a deft reference to Gottsched's inept effort to prove that Milton stole much of his material from Germany, Lessing says: "Hier will ich ihm also mit einem bessern, gegründetern Beyspiele an die Hand gehen, wie gern sich die englische Biene auf unsern blumenreichen deutschen Auen treffen lässt."[2] There follow several extracts from the

[1] Gotthold Emphraim Lessing, *Sämtliche Schriften*, ed. K. Lachmann, 3rd rev. ed. F. Muncker, 23 vols. (Stuttgart and Leipzig, 1886-1924), VIII, p. 86.
[2] *Ibid.*, VIII, p. 170.

two texts, which are almost identical. Then comes the *coup de grâce*. He playfully suggests that the reader may believe that he has made up the English version himself, and adds: "Allzuviel Ehre für mich: Nein, nein; mein Engländer existiret und heisst – *Nicholas Rowe*. Was kann Herr Wieland dafür, dass *Nicholas Rowe* schon vor vierzig und mehr Jahren gestorben ist?"[1] Lessing then proceeds to analyse the two plays carefully and shows where Wieland has departed from Rowe's text and lost in effectiveness in almost every case. This is comparative criticism in a manner which was later to become popular amongst French scholars.

Lessing was also interested in foreign criticism, and in Letter 103 he follows Joseph Warton and Diderot in making a distinction between 'le versificateur' and 'le poète'. He expresses himself on the subject of Italian literature in a review of Johann Meinhard's *Versuche über den Charakter und die Werke der besten italienischen Dichter* in letter 332. He further demonstrates his keen interest in the literary situation in other European countries in the *Hamburgische Dramaturgie* (1767-9). In the eighth and ninth pieces he enters into a discussion of Rousseau's *La nouvelle Héloise* and a comparison with a German stage adaptation, much to the disadvantage of the latter. In the eleventh and twelfth pieces he discusses at some length the reasons why the appearance of Ninus' ghost in Voltaire's *Sémiramis* is not nearly so effective as the king's ghost in *Hamlet*. Basically the difference lies in the fact that Shakespeare had an uncanny touch for bringing on his ghost in circumstances which would be credible to the spectator, whereas Voltaire brought on his ghost in daylight in front of a crowd, thus completely missing the necessary atmosphere. In this matter Lessing reveals a tendency towards historical criticism:

> Sehr wohl; das ganze Alterthum hat Gespenster geglaubt. Die dramatischen Dichter des Alterthums hatten also recht, diesen Glauben zu nutzen; wenn wir bey einem von ihnen wiederkommende Todte aufgeführet finden, so wäre es unbillig, ihm nach unsern bessern Einsichten den Process zu machen. Aber hat darum der neue, diese unsere bessere Einsichten theilende dramatische Dichter die nämliche Befugnis? Gewiss nicht.[2]

[1] *Ibid.*, VIII, p. 173.   [2] *Ibid.*, IX, p. 227.

The twelfth piece is concluded with some observations about a German translation of one of Voltaire's minor plays and the various attitudes of Frenchmen, Germans, Englishmen and Italians towards the structure of a play. Lessing comes to much the same conclusions as Schlegel; in this respect the Germans are found to be closer to the French than the English in their desire for simple plots.

Lessing considers another one of Voltaire's plays, *Zaire*, in the fifteenth and sixteenth pieces. He notes how the English, Italians and Germans have adapted it in a different manner. "Dem Welschen ist Voltaire zu kurz; uns Deutschen ist er zu lang."[1] He also sets out to prove that Voltaire modelled the character of Orosman upon that of Othello and that the result was an inferior piece of characterization on Voltaire's part. In fact Voltaire, the most distinguished contemporary representative of French classical drama, constantly comes under attack in the *Hamburgische Dramaturgie*. His tragedy *Mérope* is examined in considerable detail and compared at some length with a play of the same title by Maffei. In the course of his criticism of Voltaire's *Mérope* Lessing repeats the charge that the French playwrights actually fail to observe the spirit of the Aristotelian rules and acknowledges his debt to Schlegel by quoting the relevant passage from the *Gedanken*. This lesson is more or less the theme of the *Dramaturgie* and is tersely summed up in the final piece. "Gerade keine Nation hat die Regeln des alten Drama mehr verkannt als die Franzosen."[2]

English and Spanish drama come under close scrutiny when Lessing makes a thorough and extensive examination of John Banks' *The Unhappy Favourite; or, the Earl of Essex* and of a Spanish tragedy by an anonymous author entitled *Dar la vide por su Dama ó el Conde de Sex*. Each play is taken to represent the particular national preferences of its author, and Lessing provides lengthy extracts from each work. In contrast to the French theatre the English play is held to be full of vitality and meaning. After reproducing some scenes from Banks' drama Lessing says; "Ich, meines Theils, möchte diese Scenen lieber auch nur gedacht, als den ganzen Essex des Corneille gemacht haben. Sie sind so charac-

---

[1] Lessing, *op. cit.*, IX, pp. 249–50.   [2] *Ibid.*, X, p. 215.

teristisch, so voller Leben und Wahrheit, dass das Beste des Franzosen eine sehr armselige Figur dagegen macht."[1] We do not find in Lessing's work any surveys of foreign literature such as we found in the work of Rapin, Blair and Morhof: Lessing tended to concentrate upon individual works and draw general conclusions from them. He was obviously much more interested in the drama than in any other genres and he steadfastly remained an advocate of the Aristotelian rules as he understood them. Nevertheless he was able to appreciate the qualities of much foreign drama which did not adhere to those rules, and even if he did not go so far as to subscribe to the idea of relativity, he certainly went further in this direction than the ardent supporters of the *Anciens*. "Denn ich bin sehr überzeugt, dass kein Volk in der Welt irgendeine Gabe des Geistes vorzüglich vor andern Völkern erhalten habe."[2] Although Herder's approach to comparative literature was quite different from that of Lessing, and his first collection of *Fragmente* appeared before the *Hamburgische Dramaturgie*, Herder was definitely familiar with all of Lessing's major works and greatly admired them. No better proof of this could be given than *Funken aus der Asche eines Todten* – a collection of extracts from Lessing's works, which forms a large portion of the ninth collection of the *Humanitätsbriefe*.

We have now arrived at a period in German literature when most of the major figures were personally acquainted with Herder. In fact Herder spent two weeks with Lessing in Hamburg in February, 1770 and was cordially received. Another writer who knew both Herder and Lessing, and indeed most other prominent literary men of the day, was Friedrich Nicolai. His most important contribution to literature was his business acumen and editorial talent. He founded and edited the *Bibliothek der schönen Wissenschaften und freyen Künste* (1757-9), the *Briefe, die neueste Litteratur betreffend* (1759-65) and the *Allgemeine deutsche Bibliothek* (1765-1805). These journals played an important part in making foreign literature known to Germans. Perhaps one cannot really say that they contained much comparative literature; the reviews of foreign works generally consisted of a report about the contents rather

---

[1] Lessing, *op. cit.*, X, p. 29.   [2] *Ibid.*, X, p. 127.

than genuine criticism. Of course Lessing's contributions offered something more, as we have already seen, and Herder himself contributed to the *Allgemeine deutsche Bibliothek* many articles, which were of a more perceptive nature.

Of Nicolai's own writings little need be said here. His *Briefe über den itzigen Zustand der schönen Wissenschaften in Deutschland* (1755) consists mainly of criticism of basic faults in German writing in the past and of factionalism. He spares neither Gottsched nor the Swiss critics. The work also contains words of encouragement and advice for young German authors in the future. He repeats many of Schlegel's arguments, particularly in regard to the English theatre. Having opened with the remark, "Es wäre überhaupt zu wünschen, dass die engländische Schauspiele bei uns nicht so gering geschäzzet würden"[1] he launches a strong attack upon Gottsched and his school. Nicolai's explanation of the advantages stemming from the irregularity of the English theatre and the contrasting criticism of the French follow much the same pattern as that which we saw in Schlegel's *Gedanken*. Of course the *Gedanken* had not yet been published, but it appears that this sort of criticism of the French theatre and praise of the English theatre was quite common amongst certain German men of letters in this period. Nicolai further criticizes the French for producing the *Journal étranger*, which, he claims, demonstrates by its very title how self-centred French literature had become. He uses the occasion to plead for the intrinsic value of each national literature: in his opinion the only thing which really counts is genius: "Das Genie, die *vivida vis animi*, ist die einzige Thür zu dem Vortreflichen in den schönen Wissenschaften..."[2] He rounds off his advice to young German poets by warning them that they receive too much adulation at an early stage and contrasts their situation with that of French and English poets.

A good example of the sort of attention which foreign literature received in Nicolai's journals is Moses Mendelssohn's long review of Joseph Warton's *Essay on the Writings and Genius of Pope*, which appeared

---

[1] Friedrich Nicolai, *Briefe über den itzigen Zustand der schönen Wissenschaften in Deutschland*, ed. G. Ellinger (Berlin, 1894), p. 87.
[2] *Ibid.*, p. 146.

in the *Bibliothek der Schönen Wissenschaften* in two parts (1758-9). In the course of fifty pages Mendelssohn hardly voices an opinion of his own, but simply provides a complete summary of the contents of Warton's work. In this case one may say that the *Bibliothek* provided the Germans with some second-hand comparative literature. Although Mendelssohn was an important critic in the field of aesthetics he did not figure prominently in the area of comparative literature. The only piece which merits special attention here is letter 123 of the *Litteraturbriefe*. In a manner fairly similar to that of Lessing in his study of *Lady Johanna Gray* Mendelssohn analyses Wieland's *Clementina von Porretta* and compares it with Richardson's *Sir Charles Grandison*. His main purpose is to show how one may depict a perfect character in a novel, but not in a drama. He quotes approvingly Shaftesbury's maxim: "In a poem (whether epick or dramatick) a compleat and perfect character is the greatest Monster, and of all poetick fictions not only the least engaging, but the least moral and improving."[1] and sets out to show how unsatisfactory is the main character in *Clementina von Porretta*.

Heinrich von Gerstenberg's *Briefe über Merkwürdigkeiten der Litteratur* appeared in the summer of 1766, a few months before Herder's first collection of *Fragmente*. Gerstenberg's work contains informative letters about Thomas Warton and Spenser, Ariosto, Ossian and Percy, old Norse poetry, Don Quixote and four long letters in which he studies Shakespeare. Nor are these letters mere summaries of content: he is quite ready to express his own opinion in each matter. In the case of Spenser he entirely supports Warton's historical point of view:

> Ich verehre die Alten: aber ich mag meine Empfindungen nicht von ihnen ein-
> schränken lassen. Ist der Neuere ein Mann von Genie? Gut! er hat ein Recht auf
> meine Ehrerbietung, und ich werde mich durch eine unanständige Vergleichung
> nicht an die Gesetze der Hospitalität vergreifen.[2]

---

[1] Moses Mendelssohn, *Gesammelte Schriften*, ed. G. B. Mendelssohn, 7 vols. (Leipzig, 1843-5), IV, pt. 2, p. 144.

[2] Heinrich W. von Gerstenberg, *Briefe über Merkwürdigkeiten der Litteratur*, ed. Alexander von Weilen (Stuttgart, 1890), p. 15.

In fact Gerstenberg disagrees with Warton about the necessity for Prince Arthur to play a leading role in each episode of Spenser's epic and offers cogent reasons for his opinion. Furthermore he takes Warton to task for his criticism of Ariosto and failure to consider the Italian poet on his own terms. His determination to find out what Ariosto was trying to do and refusal to judge his work according to preconceived notions must have appealed to Herder, who often stressed this very point. "So manchen Maasstab der Dichter Einer Nation oder verschiedener Völker man aufgestellt hat, so manche vergebliche Arbeit hat man übernommen."[1] Of course Gerstenberg does not forget Warton's formal declaration of belief in historical and relativistic criticism, but he is still sceptical about Warton: "Finden Sie das? Sehr wohl! aber warum so spät?"[2]

As far as Ossian is concerned Gerstenberg, unlike Herder, was willing to recognize the possibility, even the probability that Macpherson had perpetrated a fraud. Under the pretense of having received some information from an Irishman he lists several reasons why he believes that the work is not genuine. He goes on to praise Percy's *Reliques* as highly as Herder ever praised them. Quoting one poem from the collection he says; "aber Sie haben schwerlich etwas gelesen, das von einer feinern Erfindung, von einer zärtlichern Wendung wäre, oder mehr verdiente, den schönsten Überbleibseln des griechischen Alterthums an die Seite gesetzt zu werden."[3] He also believes that no country has more riches in this respect than Denmark, and he backs up this claim with some extracts from the *Kiämpe-Viiser*, a collection of ancient lyric poetry in modern Danish translation. Gerstenberg also shows a deep respect and affection for *Don Quixote*. At first, he says, he read it as a witty piece of satire and an entertaining novel; "itzt lese ich ihn, als eine der wenigen classischen Compositionen unter den neuern, die dem Geschmacke, der Urbanität und der Weisheit des feinsten Atheniensers Ehre machen würden."[4] He then sets out to show how Cervantes' masterpiece drew its strength and character from the country in which it was written. In one of the last letters Gerstenberg demonstrates in a satirical manner worthy of Lessing,

[1] Herder, XVIII, p. 135.   [2] Gerstenberg, *op. cit.*, p. 41.
[3] *Ibid.*, p. 58.   [4] *Ibid.*, p. 258.

that the play *Double Falsehood*, published by Lewis Theobald and alleged to be one of the missing works of Shakespeare, based upon an episode in *Don Quixote*, could not possibly have come from the hand of Shakespeare.[1] The four long letters devoted to Shakespeare contain too much material to be summarized briefly here. Suffice it to say that Gerstenberg shows a deep appreciation of the great writer and points out many of his qualities with quotations from the plays. To those who complain about Shakespeare's "fehlerhaften Geschmack" he replies: "Und dreymal Schade, setze ich hinzu, dass es nicht anders seyn konnte, wenn wir ihn beständig nur auf uns, und auf unser Jahrhundert beziehen."[2]

Despite certain reservations about a few minor points of style Herder was enthusiastic about the *Briefe* from the beginning. In a letter to Scheffner dated 4th October 1766 Herder asks him if he has read the *Briefe*, and indicates by his observations that he was already familiar with the work himself. In the first part of the *Kritische Wälder* he refers to it as "eine der besten kritischen Schriften unserer Zeit."[3] and as Haym says: "Alles in Allem, so stand Herder diesen Schleswigschen Litteraturbriefen innerlich näher als den Berlinischen."[4] Apparently both writers had a parallel interest in foreign, and more particularly English and Nordic literature. Weilen believes that Herder was influenced by Gerstenberg in his revision of the first two collections of *Fragmente*, but he admits that it is difficult to prove this theory. Haym demonstrates how their interest in Ossian and Shakespeare coincided, and speaking of letters 8 and 14-18 he says: "Ein Seitenstück zu jenem bildet der *Auszug aus einem Briefwechsel über Ossian und die Lieder alter Völker:* auf diese bezieht sich der Aufsatz über Shakespeare."[5] He goes on to explain how Herder's essay on Shakespeare was originally intended to be a contribution to a continuation of the *Briefe*. Indeed, Herder admits his debt to Gerstenberg in the first version of the essay which opens with the statement:

[1] In his introduction to the *Briefe* Weilen claims that Gerstenberg was the first critic to ascribe the play to Theobald himself. As T. R. Lounsbury shows, in *The Text of Shakespeare*, Theobald was already assumed to be the author by the *Grub Street Journal* in 1730.
[2] Gerstenberg, *op. cit.*, p. 125.   [3] Herder, III, p. 25.
[4] Haym, *op. cit.*, I, p. 428.   [5] *Ibid.*

Ja, mein Herr, Sie können es, wenn Ihnen dieser Brief gedruckt vor Augen kommt, Sie können es Jemanden glauben, der kein Recht hat, Ihnen als Freund, und keine Lust Ihnen als Schriftsteller zu schmeicheln, dass mir Shakespear, der grosse Shakespear in Ihren wenigen Briefen über ihn mehr erschienen ist, als in so manchen Vorreden, Noten, Versuchen und Lobreden so mancher seiner Landsleute; so Viel Vortrefliches diese über ihn gesschrieben.[1]

Herder also uses the occasion to praise Gerstenberg for his treatment of Spenser, Milton, Cervantes and scaldic poetry. Gerstenberg's contribution to comparative literature has been completely overshadowed by that of Herder, but Herder was amongst the first to point out the injustice of the neglect of Gerstenberg. In the seventh collection of the *Humanitäts-briefe* he wrote about the *Briefe über Merkwürdigkeiten der Litteratur* as, "eine Sammlung Briefe, die weit mehr Aufmerksamkeit verdient, als sie erlangt.[2]"

All the German contributions to comparative literature which we have so far discussed have consisted either of historical surveys of European literature or of analysis of selected works from different European countries. We now turn to another kind of work, one of the earliest reference guides in this field of studies. In 1764 Philipp Ernst Bertram published his *Entwurf einer Geschichte der Gelahrtheit;* it consists of an impressive set of bibliographies covering the whole range of human knowledge. The section which is of immediate interest to us is entitled *Von der Dichtkunst* and contains, on average, a ten-page bibliography of the works of Italian, French, Spanish, German, English and Dutch literature. To each of these Bertram provides a short introduction giving an outline of the historical development of writing in the country in question. In most cases he includes a brief personal evaluation of the various periods. He believes in the idea of a golden age in each country, with long periods of build-up and anti-climax. Of the Italian renaissance he says: "Dieser schöne Zeitpunct war von keiner langen Dauer. Die Italienische Dichtkunst hatte hierinn keinen Vorzug vor andern."[3] It is perhaps amusing to note that he blames the French for their misrepresen-

[1] Herder, v, p. 232.   [2] *Ibid.*, XVIII, p. 31.
[3] Philipp Ernst Bertram, *Entwurf einer Geschichte der Gelahrtheit* (Halle, 1764), p. 318.

tation of Spanish literature and considers that it would be an insult to say that Spain had already enjoyed her golden age.

Bertram is willing to acknowledge the backwardness of German letters in comparison to other nations, and offers as an explanation "die immerwährende Unruhen." He is, however, reluctant to pass judgement upon contemporary writers: "Ich will anjetzo lieber furchtsam seyn, als mir herbe Urtheile zuwegebringen."[1] He has particularly kind words for English literature, which is distinguished by "die originelle Denkungsart, Stärke im Ausdruck, Pracht in Beschreibungen und Reichthum in Bildern."[2] He singles out Shakespeare, Cowley, Waller and Milton for special commendation and many other writers have laudatory adjectives prefixed to their names. Of Shakespeare he says: "Sein Genie ist gross, erhaben, und kennt keine Schranken und Regeln."[3] All in all the English are granted an advantage over other European nations. The main value of Bertram's work, however, does not lie in his opinions, but rather in the bibliographies themselves. As Lempicki tells us, Bertram "lieferte ein vorzügliches bibliographisches Kompendium, aus dem der junge Herder fleissig exzerpierte."[4], but unfortunately he fails to provide any evidence for this statement. In any case there can be no doubt that Bertram was a pioneer in this form of comparative literature.

Johann Nicolaus Meinhard played a different, but no less important auxiliary role which deserves to be mentioned. He originally planned a library of world literature in German translation, but owing to a lack of public enthusiasm he had to curtail the project. Nevertheless his *Versuche über den Charakter und die Werke der besten italienischen Dichter* (1763) was instrumental in bringing Italian literature to the attention of the German public. As Helmut Rehder informs us; "meistens beschränkt er sich auf eine strenge, fast monotone Objektivität der Beschreibung, und nur in Bezug auf ästhetische, künstlerische Werte klingt gelegentlich ein persönliches Urteil an, – das Bekenntnis zu einem klaren, nüchternen, rationalen Klassizismus."[5] In addition to the translations from Italian

---

[1] Bertram, *op. cit.*, p. 364.   [2] *Ibid.*, p. 372.
[3] *Ibid.*, p. 373.   [4] Lempicki, *op. cit.*, p. 210.
[5] Helmut Rehder, *Johann Nicolaus Meinhard und seine Übersetzungen*, Illinois Studies in Language and Literature, XXXVII, no. 2 (Urbana, 1953), p. 9.

works he produced a German version of Henry Home's *Elements of Criticism* and of several minor works from French, Spanish and English literature. Amongst these translations was a work of considerable significance for comparative literature – Melchiorre Cesarotti's *Ragiona-mento sopra l'origine e i progressi dell'arte poetica* (1762). Meinhard's version appeared in the *Bibliothek der schönen Wissenschaften* in 1766, and although there is no definite proof that Herder read it we know that he was a regular reader of that journal. Cesarotti was a firm advocate of historical relativism. "Jedes Volk hat seine Religion, seine Gesetze, Sitten, Mey-nungen, Gebräuche, seinen Wahn. Wer in diesem Chaos Grundsätze, Zusammenhang, Vernunft suchen wollte, würde sich sehr irren."[1] In rejecting any standard rules, including implicitly those of Aristotle, Meinhard reminds us, "dass die Natur den Saamen der Poesie über alle Länder auf gleiche Weise vertheilt (hat) ... (und) dass, nach der ver-schiednen Art des Erdreichs, die Pflanze auf verschiedne Arten sprosset und wächst."[2] Herder used similar imagery when he put forward the same argument, as, for instance, in the eighth collection of the *Humani-tätsbriefe;* "Flechte, Moos, Farrenkraut und die reichste Gewürzblume; jedes blühet an seiner Stelle in Gottes Ordnung."[3]

Cesarotti also stresses the vital need for genius and individuality, and this leads Rehder to remark: "In Bezug auf die Wertung individueller und volkstümlicher Eigenheiten der Literatur scheint Cesarotti die Denkweise Herders fast um ein Jahrzehnt vorausgenommen zu haben."[4] Whether Herder derived any of his ideas from Cesarotti's work is open to question, but we can be sure that he was familiar with some of Mein-hard's translations. In fact he wrote an inscription in a copy of the *Versuche* owned by his friend Woldemar Dietrich von Budberg, who was a former pupil of Meinhard. In the first *Kritisches Wäldchen* Herder expressed a high opinion of Meinhard's talents:

Dieser würdige Mann besass so viel Gabe des Ausdrucks, die Poesie einer fremden Sprache in die unsere zu prosaisiren, oder wenn man lieber will, die Prose unsrer Sprache so geschickt zum einfältigen Adel der Poesie eines fremden Ausdrucks zu

¹ Rehder, *op. cit.*, p. 54.   ² *Ibid.*
³ Herder, XVIII, p. 138.   ⁴ Rehder, *op. cit.*, p. 57.

erheben, dass ihn die Muse unsres Vaterlandes bestimmt zu haben schien, der Mund fremder Nationen unter uns zu werden.[1]

For some unknown reason Herder evidently revised his opinion over the years, and in the *Humanitätsbriefe* he speaks of "Meinhards schwacher Versuch über die Italianischen Dichter."[2]

Although Cesarotti was an Italian and Meinhard was no more than a translator we have seen that there were plenty of German writers who concerned themselves with foreign literature during the latter part of the seventeenth and the first half of the eighteenth century. This interest was no doubt due in part to the generally acknowledged backwardness of German literature: German writers felt that they had to look to other countries for models. Gottsched and his followers turned towards France, whilst the Swiss critics, Schlegel and Lessing believed that the Germans had more affinities with the English. Time was on the side of the latter and the attention of German writers was increasingly directed towards England. Yet there was one point upon which all parties were more or less agreed; they all held to the classical rules, and in the dispute about the comparative merits of French and English drama (and the debate centred round the theatre) each side claimed that its favourite had followed more truly Aristotle's precepts. This situation lasted until Herder and Gerstenberg appeared on the scene, and severely limited the possibility of historical and relativistic criticism.

Schlegel and Lessing may have believed that each nation had an equal chance of producing great literature, but they still judged all literary works by a set standard and made little allowance for national differences. Only in Bodmer could one find the true beginnings of historical criticism. Although German writers were probably more interested, as a group, in foreign literature than their French or English counterparts, we have seen in previous chapters that the latter also looked beyond their national boundaries. Thus such activity cannot be regarded as a specifically German contribution to comparative literature. There is, how-

[1] Herder, III, p. 126.
[2] *Ibid.*, XVIII, p. 137.

ever, in French and English criticism nothing similar to Lessing's extensive analysis and comparison of two works upon the same theme in different languages, and nothing to vie with Bertram's bibliographical compendium. In the next chapter we shall see how Herder built upon this solid foundation of comparative literary criticism in Germany.

CHAPTER V

HERDER AS COMPARATIST

In the last chapter we saw how some of the German critics of the seventeenth and eighteenth centuries interested themselves in comparative literature. We observed that one of the main reasons for this interest in foreign works was the dismal state of German literature. Indeed, throughout the course of this study we have seen how the desire to support and improve the state of letters in their own country has impelled writers to pass beyond national boundaries. This was already the case with Du Bellay in 1549, and Herder felt the same sort of pressure more than two centuries later. Sir Isaiah Berlin summed this up neatly in a recent article about Herder; "He suffered that mixture of envy, humiliation, admiration, resentment, and defiant pride which backward peoples feel toward advanced ones, members of one social class towards those who belong to a higher rung in the hierarchy."[1] Berlin takes some pains to point out that Herder's nationalism was not political, but it certainly affected his attitude towards the study of foreign literature.

This fact is apparent in the earliest of his writings which may be considered to belong to the field of comparative literature, and nationalism remained a dominant influence throughout his life. He opens the first collection of *Fragmente über die neuere Deutsche Litteratur* (1766) with the statement that he is providing a continuation of the *Litteraturbriefe*, although he really has a much more extensive work in mind – "ein Werk, das sich den Plan vorzeichnete zu einem ganzen und vollendeten Gemälde über die Litteratur, wo kein Zug ohne Bedeutung auf das Ganze

[1] Sir Isaiah Berlin, "Herder," *Encounter*, Vol. xxv, No. 1, p. 42.

wäre..."[1] Herder's purpose, however, was not merely to produce a general history of literature; his aims were more specific and he laid them out so clearly on this occasion that it would be unwise to abbreviate or attempt to paraphrase them:

> Man lasse mich meinen Traum verfolgen! Diesem allgemeinen und einzigen Werke müste eine Geschichte der Litteratur zum Grunde liegen, auf die es sich stüzzte. Auf welcher Stuffe befindet sich diese Nation? und zu welcher könnte und sollte sie kommen? Was sind ihre Talente, und wie ist ihr Geschmack? Wie ihr äusserer Zustand in den Wissenschaften und Künsten? Warum sind sie bisher noch nicht höher gekommen, und wodurch könnte ihr Geist zum Aufschwunge Freiheit und Begeisterung erhalten? Alsdenn ruffe der Geschichtschreiber der Litteratur aus: "Wohlan! Landesleute, diese Bahn laufet, und jene Abwege und Steine vermeidet: so weit habt ihr noch, um hierinn den Kranz des Zieles zu erreichen!" Man stelle ihnen die Alten als Vorläufer, die Nachbarn als Nebenbuhler vor, und suche die Triebfeder des Nationalstolzes so rege zu machen, als man das Nationalgenie untersucht hat. Kurz! eine solche Geschichte suche das, was sie bey den Alten war, zu werden: die Stimme der Patriotischen Weisheit und die Verbesserin des Volks.[2]

Herder was unable to achieve this vast goal in the three collections of *Fragmente*, but the fault was not entirely his own. As Suphan shows in his introduction, Herder's publisher, Hartknoch, managed to dissuade him from making any sweeping changes or additions to the *Fragmente* when they were re-issued. At the end of the second collection Herder announced his plans for the third collection, which never appeared in the proposed form. "Wer die Fortsezzung dieser Parallele wünscht; der erwarte im dritten Theil etwas von unsern Römern, Engländern und Franzosen: und nachdem alle Schulden abgetragen sind, wollen wir unser eignes Kapital berechnen und fragen: wozu wirs anwenden könnten."[3] In fact this plan was not fulfilled until almost thirty years later when Herder wrote the seventh and eighth collections of the *Humanitätsbriefe*. It is surely more than a coincidence that he divides the letters in these two collections into nine groups of *Fragmente*, a division which does not occur in the other collections of the *Humanitätsbriefe*. His main idea

[1] Herder, I, p. 140.   [2] *Ibid.*, I, p. 140.   [3] *Ibid.*, I, p. 355.

about the purpose of studying foreign literature did not change during those thirty years. Already in the *Fragmente* Herder finds that the establishment of national identity plays a key role in the production of great literature. He asks himself whence certain foreign authors draw their strength;

> Warum haben Shakespear und Hudibras: Swift und Fielding sich so sehr das Gefühl ihrer Nation zu eigen gemacht? Weil sie die Fundgruben ihrer Sprache durchforschet, und ihren Humour mit Idiotismen, jeden nach seiner Art und seinem Maas, gepaart haben. Warum vertheidigen die Engländer ihren Shakespear, selbst wenn er sich unter die *Concetti* und Wortspiele verirrt? – Eben diese *Concetti*, die er mit Wortspielen vermählt, sind Früchte, die nicht in ein anderes Clima entführt werden können. Der Dichter wuste den Eigensinn der Sprache so mit dem Eigensinn seines Wizzes zu paaren, dass sie für einander gemacht zu seyn scheinen.[1]

This is the foundation upon which Herder's relativism rests and it shows the path which German writers must follow if they wish to achieve greatness; and Herder certainly wishes it for them. A writer should attempt to represent the thoughts and actions or the people amongst whom he lives and steep himself in their culture. Indeed, this should not even be a conscious process; and if he succeeds in this his work cannot be set beside that of a writer from a different culture for the purpose of qualitative comparison.

As we have already seen, this preoccupation with indigenous culture is not an altogether original aspect of Herder's work. Most of the critics who supported the idea of relativity, from Du Bellay and Daniel to Voltaire and the Warton brothers, insisted in varying degrees upon the necessity for each people to have their own literature and upon the futility of attempting to import a style of writing from some other country. Dubos and Montesquieu had dealt with such matters at some length.[2] Herder simply provided a more complete and sophisticated

---

[1] Herder, I, p. 163.

[2] Although Dubos and Montesquieu are probably the best known Frenchmen who wrote about the significance of national character and physical surroundings in literature they were by no means the first. Professor R. W. Southern cites an example from a letter of Pierre de Celle c. 1160, where he describes Englishmen in the following manner: "Your island is

version of the familiar argument and used it for the same purpose for which we have seen it used before – to promote and encourage the national literature of the critic who is writing. In this connection the study of foreign literature serves to illustrate how other peoples have succeeded in expressing their natural character in literary works. Although the Germans may learn much from the experience of other nations the purpose of comparative criticism is definitely not to enable them to emulate their neighbours. It is rather to show them how they are different and must endeavour to develop along their own lines.

According to Herder the critic's job is to understand rather than to judge. The eighty-eighth letter of the *Humanitätsbriefe* contains a concise summary of his position:

> Wie ganzen Nationen Eine Sprache eigen ist, so sind ihnen auch gewisse Lieblings-gänge der Phantasie, Wendungen und Objecte der Gedanken, kurz ein Genius eigen, der sich, unbeschadet jeder einzelnen Verschiedenheit, in den beliebtesten Werken ihres Geistes und Herzens ausdruckt. Sie in diesem angenehmen Irrgarten zu belauschen, den Proteus zu fesseln und redend zu machen, den man gewöhnlich Nationalcharakter nennt und der sich gewiss nich weniger in Schriften als in Ge-bräuchen und Handlungen der Nation äussert; dies ist eine hohe und feine Philo-sophie. In den Werken der Dichtkunst d.i. Einbildungskraft und der Empfindungen wird sie am sichersten geübet, weil in diesen die ganze Seele der Nation sich am freiesten zeiget.[1]

Herder goes on to say that the critic must also take temporal consider-ations into account; each age has its own peculiar tone, "und es giebt ein eignes Vergnügen, diese im Gegensatz mit andern Zeiten treffend zu

surrounded by water, and not unnaturally, its inhabitants are affected by the nature of the element in which they live. Unsubstantial fantasies slide easily into their minds. They think their dreams to be visions, and their visions to be divine. We cannot blame them, for such is the nature of their land. I have often noticed that the English are greater dreamers than the French, and the reason is that their brains, being moist, are easily affected by wind in the stomach, and they imagine that the impressions which arise from their animal nature are spiritual experiences. It is different in France, which is not so wet or windy, and where the mountains are of stone and the earth is weighted down with iron." *The Listener*, Vol. LXXVI., No. 1986, p. 526.
[1] Herder, XVIII, p. 58.

charakterisiren."[1] He also explains how he finds himself in an extraordinarily advantageous position, for he can look back on the best efforts of writers in the orient, Greece, Rome, Italy, Spain and France. Describing poetry as "die Blüthe des menschlichen Geistes" he says; "so, dünkt mich, ist der glücklich, dem diese Blüthe vom Gipfel des Stammes der aufgeklärtesten Nation zu brechten vergönnt ist."[2] This letter is especially interesting since it opens with a confession which seems to undermine much of what Herder does in the rest of the seventh and eighth collections. He emphasizes the great diversity within each country and period and expresses doubt about the possibility of any valid generalizations. There follows a statement which was written, I believe, in a spirit of genuine humility and was not meant as an arrogant reference to other critics: "Die Poesie der Italiener, der Spanier, der Franzosen, wie viel, wie mancherlei begreift sie in sich! und wie wenig denket, ja wie wenig kennet der sie oft, der sie am wortreichsten charakterisiret!"[3]

Such a contradiction is not unusual in Herder's works; just as he was consistent in holding to most of his theories throughout his writing career, so he was consistent in contradicting some of them in practice. In spite of his good intentions he did not always restrict himself to appreciative criticism. In the last chapter we saw how the tide turned against Gottsched and the proponents of French classicism, and German writers generally became severely critical in regard to French literature. Many of them attempted to focus the attention of their countrymen upon English literature instead. From his earliest days Herder sympathized with this trend; in this respect two pieces which he originally intended to include in the *Fragmente* are, as Suphan points out, doubly important. *Haben wir eine Französische Bühne?* and *Vom Brittischen Geschmack in Schauspielen* were not actually published during Herder's lifetime, but they represent his first views upon the theatre and they were written before the appearance of the *Hamburgische Dramaturgie*.

In the first piece he gives a critical account of the French theatre with its "canonische Regelmässigkeit" and expresses in a milder tone the same wish which Lessing was to utter in the following year – that the French

[1] *Ibid.*   [2] *Ibid.*, XVIII, p. 57.   [3] *Ibid.*

methods and rules had never been introduced into Germany. In the second piece he shows more interest in the future of the German theatre than in the intrinsic merits of the French or English theatre. He is, however, far more sympathetic towards the English stage, and particularly Shakespeare, since it has more to offer to the German character. "Wir müssen zuerst den Deutschen etwas zu sehen verschaffen: hiezu sind die Franzosen unbrauchbar; aber die Engländer? und Shakespear? – Ja sie geben sehr viel zu sehen; aber uns Deutschen wirklich zu viel."[1]

In these early writings we can already trace an incipient conflict between Herder's relativistic ideas and his concern for the growth of native German literature. In later works the latter interest led him into making value judgements about foreign literature. The second *Kritisches Wäldchen* (1769) contains evidence to prove that he was already formulating his relativistic ideas in this period of his life.

> So wie der oberste Richter allwissend seyn muss, um gleichsam die eigenthümliche Moralität eines jeden Herzens zu kennen: so sey (man erlaube mir die kleine Blasphemie vom Gleichnisse!) so sey der Richter über Zeiten und Völker, auch des Geschmacks dieser Zeiten und Völker kundig, oder er greift blind in den Loostopf der Jahrhunderte, um nichts als ein mageres kritisches Regelchen herauszulangen.[2]

Despite this statement Herder still demonstrates either inability or reluctance to appreciate French literature in the *Journal meiner Reise im Jahr 1769* – the same year as that in which the foregoing statement of principle appeared. Speaking of his literary plans for the future he says; "Dazu will ich eine beständige Lecture der Menschheitsschriften, in denen Deutschland jetzt seine Periode anfängt, und Frankreich, das ganz Convention und Blendwerk ist, die seinige verlebt hat, unterhalten."[3] In another passage he not only declares that France's great period of literary activity is past but even questions the originality of the writers in the golden period under Louis xiv. He appears to deliberately denigrate the French achievements; perhaps with some justification, but he exaggerates the extent of indebtedness to Spain and Italy, thereby overshadowing the genuine French elements in the various masterpieces.

[1] *Ibid.*, II, p. 233. [2] *Ibid.*, III, pp. 233-4. [3] Herder, IV, p. 367.

109

A few pages further on he returns to the attack and tries to show how pernicious is the French mania for "Galanterie". "Immer bemüht, nicht Wahrheit der Empfindung und Zährtlichkeit zu schildern; sondern schöne Seite derselben, Art sich auszudrücken, Fähigkeit erobern zu können..."[1] Herder singles out Fontenelle as an example and declares that he would have been a really great writer if he had devoted all the energy which he wasted on external polish to the content of his works. His French qualities apparently crippled him as a writer. "Wo ist Genie? Wahrheit? Stärke? Tugend?"[2] Herder asks himself about French literature, and the answer is – nowhere.

When we examined Voltaire's contributions to comparative literature we found that he still harboured ideas about a perfect epic and an ideal theatre in spite of his lip service to the idea of relativity. For him the purpose of studying the English theatre, for example, was to discover any qualities which might profitably be incorporated into the French theatre. Herder appears to follow a similar path in the *Journal meiner Reise*. After criticizing the French people for their fastidiousness and unhealthy emphasis on etiquette he says:

> Welche freiere Natur haben da die Engländer, nur auch freilich übertrieben! und was könnten wir Deutsche uns für eine schöne mitlere Laufbahn nehmen! Die Komödie vom Italiener, die Tragedie vom Engländer, in beiden die Französische Feile hinten nach, welch ein neues Theater![3]

In this section Herder does not mention what the specifically German contribution will be and it appears as if he is not altogether aware of the dangers of being able to look back upon the literary efforts of so many nations. As we have seen, earlier critics in France, England and Germany were apprehensive about this matter. For instance, Sir William Temple, the defender of the ancients against the moderns, warned against the slavish imitation of the ancients and feared that native genius might be stifled. Few relativists would claim that all contact with foreign literature is harmful and that the native genius of each country should be permitted to develop on its own without the corruption of outside

---

[1] *Ibid.*, IV, p. 425.   [2] *Ibid.*, IV, p. 427.   [3] *Ibid.*, IV, p. 433.

influences. Herder always maintained that the Germans could derive benefit from the study of all foreign literature. Nevertheless it is surprising to find him so enthusiastic about copying the various traits of English, Italian and French literature when the battle to discredit Gottsched and free the Germans from the influence of the French had been so recently won.

Here we come up against another of those inconsistencies in Herder's work which make it so difficult to give a summary of his ideas. One always risks leaving oneself open to refutation by a quotation from some part of his writings which one had overlooked. If one looks for clear categorical statements of opinion in a writer, then Saintsbury's criticism of Herder is justified: Herder was unable to express all his important ideas in one concise work. Often there are contradictions even within one work, and these would inevitably have been greatly multiplied if he had tried to concentrate everything into one great work. Although dogmatic statements abound in Herder's works he was not on the whole a dogmatic thinker. If he found some new idea and wished to pursue it further he would not allow himself to be confined by any previous thoughts which he may have had upon the matter in question. Thus one should not turn to his works so much for instruction as for stimulation, and this is the reason why many of these works are still of interest to the twentieth century reader.

Herder's varying attitude towards comparative literature affords us an excellent opportunity to illustrate these vacillations of opinion. As we have just observed he was on occasion extremely enthusiastic about literary works passing beyond national frontiers and was delighted at the prospect of German literature borrowing a great deal from neighbouring countries. In the prize essay *Über die Wirkung der Dichtkunst auf die Sitten der Völker in alten und neuen Zeiten* (1778) he put forward quite a different point of view. In the middle of a general survey of European literary history we find the following comments:

> Je mehr die Länder zusammen rückten, die Kultur der Wissenschaften, die Gemeinschaft der Stände, Provinzen, Königreiche und Welttheile zunahm; je mehr also, wie alle Litteratur, so auch Poesie an Raum und Oberfläche die Würkung gewann, desto mehr verlohr sie an Eindrang, Tiefe und Bestimmtheit. In engen Staaten,

III

bei kleinen Völkern, ihren einförmigen Sitten, engem und jedem einzelnen Gliede anschaulichem Interesse, bei Thaten, wo jeder Richter und Zeuge seyn konnte, hatte sie gewürkt und geblühet; jetzt ihre Flamme in Staaten und Schimmer auf der Erde ... Endlich und am meisten, wenn die Sitten und Herzen aller sogenannten gebildeten Völker allmälig abgegriffene Münzen werden da die Dichtkunst nur mit Schaustücken zu thun haben soll: wie anders, als dass diese auch so werde? fein ausgearbeitet, bequem und schön, aber meistens ohne Inhalt und Werth der alten engen Nationaldichtkunst.[1]

This is more than a mere temporary aberration on Herder's part; he returns to this theme several times in the course of his historical account of the development of Italian, French, English and German literature. He even doubts seriously that society has been greatly benefited by the invention of printing, and even if it has, literature has definitely suffered. "Die Buchdruckerei hat viel Gutes gestiftet; der Dichtkunst hat sie viel von ihrer lebendigen Würkung geraubet."[2] Much of the material and many of the arguments in this essay Herder used again later in the seventh and eighth collections of the *Humanitätsbriefe*.

In another prize essay, *Ursachen des gesunknen Geschmacks bei den verschiednen Völkern, da er geblühet* (1775) it initially appears as if Herder has found a way to reconcile these different views about comparative literature. He distinguishes between "Genie" and "Geschmack": the former is the essential ingredient of any great literature and it must be a completely natural growth. It cannot be transplanted from one people to another. "Geschmack" is valuable only when it is added to "Genie" and improvements in taste may presumably come from any sources which are available.

> Geschmack ist nur Ordnung im Gebrauch der Geniekräfte, und ist also ohne Genie ein Unding. Im Gegentheil, je mehr Kräfte ein Genie hat, je rascher die Kräfte würken, desto mehr ist der Mentor des guten Geschmacks nöthig, damit sich die Kräfte nicht selbst einander überwältigen, zerrütten, und im Falle der Übermacht auch andre gute Kräfte zertrümmern.[3]

This seems to leave an area open, in which advantage may be drawn from the study of literary taste in other nations. In the course of the

---

[1] Herder, VIII, pp. 413-14.   [2] *Ibid.*, VIII, p. 411.   [3] *Ibid.*, v, p. 602.

essay, however, Herder lays great stress upon native genius which develops its own taste. He criticizes Italian and French writers for being too imitative and explains how their greatest literary geniuses lived before the time of Pope Leo x and Louis xiv. The conclusion of the essay leaves some doubt about the usefulness of looking for examples in foreign literature:

> Wir sind geboren, Glückseligkeit der Menschen zu schaffen: Genies schafft der Schöpfer, und aus Genies bildet sich der Geschmack von selbst. Wir müssen nur, wie Ärzte oder Hebammen (nach Sokrates Gleichniss), der immer schaffenden, bildenden, regelnden und wieder zerstörenden Natur folgen.[1]

However confusing these theoretical statements may be Herder was in fact an ardent practitioner of comparative literature. The introduction to the fourth book of the *Volkslieder* (1778) dispels any doubts about the value of the undertaking and makes the purpose quite clear:

> Dass wir mehr Völker des Erdbodens kennen, als die Alten kannten: ist Vorzug unsrer Zeit, und wie man sie auch kennen gelernt? was sie oder wir sonst dabei verlohren? die Känntniss selbst, die daher aufgekeimt, ist gut: die Charte der Menschheit ist ungeheur verbreitet. Was war Erdkunde unter Griechen und Römern? und was ist sie jetzt?
>
> Wie aber nun diese Völker, die Brüder unsrer Menschheit kennen? blos von aussen, durch Fratzenkupferstiche und Nachrichten, die den Kupferstichen gleichen, oder von innen? als Menschen, die Sprache, Seele, Empfindungen haben? unsre Brüder! – Kein Mensch wird in einem Philosophischen Jahrhunderte, wo nichts als Menschlichkeit gekannt, geliebt, und gebildet wird, die Nothwendigkeit und Vorzug der letztern Känntnisse läugnen.[2]

Herder then elaborates upon the manner in which the character of a people is reflected in all its facets in their folksongs. In offering his fellow-countrymen selections from the folksongs of different nations Herder believes that he can acquaint them with the true character of other peoples.

Such an aim appears to be somewhat in conflict with the historical approach to criticism, which Herder advocates elsewhere in his works. In

---

[1] *Ibid.*, v, p. 648.   [2] *Ibid.*, xxv, p. 81.

Auch eine Philosophie der Geschichte (1774) he takes a firm stand in favour of historical criticism and claims that one must take the customs and culture of a people into account when judging their works of art. Thus Winckelmann is criticized for ranking Egyptian art below that of Greece, since he failed to recognize the completely different environments in Egypt and in Greece. Herder also takes Wood, Webb, Newton and Voltaire to task for the same mistake.[1] In the essay on Shakespeare (1772) he actually provides an example of what he has in mind. He claims that Shakespeare simply cannot be judged by the dramatical standards of ancient Greece; any serious study of Shakespeare's work must be based upon a knowledge of the people for whom he was writing.

> Es wird allein erste und letzte Frage: "wie ist der Boden? worauf ist er zubereitet? was ist in ihn gesäet? was sollte er tragen können?" – und Himmel! wie weit hier von Griechenland weg! Geschichte, Tradition, Sitten, Religion, Geist der Zeit, des Volks, der Rührung, der Sprache – wie weit von Griechenland weg![2]

Where, we may ask, are we supposed to begin? Logically we appear to be going around in a circle. We cannot truly know the merits of a writer unless we know something about the environment in which he wrote, and yet it is through the same writer that we are expected to learn something about the people amongst whom he lived. In defence of Herder it must be said that one is rarely faced in practice with such an intractable logical problem. Other sources of information are usually available and any knowledge which we may have, for example, about Greek culture will no doubt be useful when we consider the works of a Greek writer. Conversely the works of that Greek author may well add to our knowledge and improve our understanding of Greek culture.

The purpose of Herder's collection of folksongs was not, however, merely to inform the Germans about the nature of their neighbours in Europe. The nationalistic element is here, just as it is in most of the other works which we have mentioned so far. In the introduction to the first part of the *Volkslieder* Herder is perfectly frank about his intentions:

[1] Herder, v, p. 491.
[2] *Ibid.*, v, p. 217.

Ich erscheine mit Armuth, blos damit ich andre, reichere Mitbürger, Länder, Gegenden, Bibliotheken, Provinzen wecke! Ich bringe eine Handvoll Wasser dar, deren ich mich beinah selbst schäme, und stelle die einem nachbarlichen Gastmal von Fülle und Wohlstand gegenüber: sollte ich keinen meiner Mitbrüder, Deutsche, Landsleute, Landsfreunde finden, denen ich damit Eifersucht und Galle rege, dass sie sich aufmachen, und voll edeln Zorns, Rache und Freude, (ich weiss, ich wünsche und hoffe es!) mich wie weit! wie weit! übertreffen![1]

The essay *Von Ähnlichkeit der mittlern englischen und deutschen Dichtkunst* (1777), which was originally intended as an introduction to the *Volkslieder* is imbued with the same spirit. In spite of the title there is not much actual comparison of English and German literature. The true subject of Herder's inquiry is much more specific: "hier ist aber eben die Frage, warum wir keine Shakespeare und Spenser gehabt haben?"[2] The answer which he provides here is that the Germans have failed to gather or even pay attention to their folksongs, whereas authors like Chaucer, Shakespeare and Spenser have drawn freely upon such material in England.

Herder was always fascinated by this question, and it was, I believe, one of the main spurs which drove him to the study of comparative literature. On many occasions he confronted the problem in a more general form; a typical and especially clear instance is the essay *Ursachen des gesunknen Geschmacks*. At the beginning he sets himself the task of discovering why "der Geschmack, die schöne Gabe des Himmels" has only flourished in a few places and for limited periods of time. "Woher nun diese Wellen auf dem grossen Meer des Zeitraums? Aus Ursachen von innen oder von aussen? Wer lehret uns das grosse Naturgesetz der Veränderungen des Geschmacks aus der Geschichte?"[3] Herder was, of course, by no means the first person to consider these questions; as we have already observed, Dubos dealt with them in some detail sixty years earlier and attributed the varying levels of culture to differences in geography and climate. Herder did not arrive at any such positivistic solution. He was able to explain why each golden age was limited in time and how decline set in, but he did not find a satisfactory explanation for

[1] Herder, xxv, p. 9.   [2] *Ibid.*, ix, p. 524.   [3] *Ibid.*, v, p. 599.

the appearance of these fruitful periods in the first place. Apparently it all depends upon "Genies", and hence ultimately upon divine will:

> Kann nun kein Mensch Genies bewürken (sie keimen aus höhern und mehrern Veranlassungen oft sehr misslicher Umstände hervor): so, sieht man, sind auch die goldenen Zeitalter des Geschmacks nie ganz Eines Menschen Wille. Sie folgen und richten sich nach jenen. Sie sind in der Geschichte des Menschlichen Geschlechts, wie die konsonen Punkte der Saite: es müssen Dissonanzen zwischen liegen und auf jenen heben sich diese.[1]

Herder believes that this natural law also accounts for the fact that great men come in groups; "sie sind alle zusammen nichts als konsoner Punkt einer Saite... die Menschliche Seele kommt in den Wohlklang."[2] He simply accepts this phenomenon and hopes that Germany is working towards a "Zeitalter des hohen Philosophischen Geschmacks".[3]

Herder returned to this problem again in the seventh and eighth collections of the *Humanitätsbriefe*. At the beginning of letter 81 he presents the question in almost identical form:

> Wie? kann man fragen, blühet diese schöne Blume der Humanität, Poesie in Denkart, Sitten und Sprache nicht überall und allezeit gleich glücklich? Und wenn zu ihrem Aufkommen ein besondrer boden eine eigene Pflege und Witterung gehöret; welches ist dieser Boden, diese Witterung und Pflege? Oder wenn sie mit jeder Zeit, unter einem andern Himmelsstrich auch ihre Gestalt und Farbe verändern muss; welches ist das Gesetz dieser Veränderung? geht sie ins Bessere oder Schlechtere über?[4]

The ostensible purpose of the whole undertaking, Herder's largest single venture into the field of comparative literature, is to provide answers to these questions. By the end of the eighth collection, however, Herder has advanced no farther than he did in *Ursachen des gesunknen Geschmacks*, and his attention seems to have switched to a different matter. The only general rule which he deduces from his relativistic survey of European literature is that German literature has a great future ahead of it. The

---

[1] Herder, v, p. 645.   [2] *Ibid.*
[3] *Ibid.*, v, p. 647.   [4] *Ibid.*, xviii, pp. 5-6.

second half of the eighth collection is devoted almost entirely to the German muse and a nationalistic tone predominates. We have seen how nationalism and relativism were linked together in earlier critics from Du Bellay onwards, and Herder follows the same path. The tendency which we have noted in the introduction to the *Volkslieder* becomes more pronounced in the *Humanitätsbriefe*.

Indeed, the nationalistic spirit waxes so strong that it seriously interferes with the theory of relativity. In the later letters Herder significantly fails to practise what he is preaching. According to the relativist point of view it is a serious error to compare writers from different nations for the purpose of ranking one above the other. They simply cannot be judged by the same standard. We have seen how Herder subscribed to this opinion on many occasions: nothing could be clearer than his statement in letter 107:

> So manchen Maasstab der Dichter Einer Nation oder verschiedener Völker man aufgestellt hat, so manche vergebliche Arbeit hat man übernommen. Jeder schätzt und ordnet sie nach seinen Lieblingsbegriffen, nach der Art, wie Er sie kennen lernte, nach der Wirkung, die Der und Jener auf ihn machte. Der gebildete Mensch trägt, wie sein Ideal der Vollkommenheit, so auch seinen Maasstab diese zu erreichen in sich, den er nicht gern mit einem fremden vertauschet.[1]

Yet he indulges in just such comparison in the eighth collection. Letter 102 is particularly revealing in this respect. Herder starts off with a general defense of the Germans against the charge that they are "ganz Charakterlos":

> Vergleicht unsre Deutsche Minnesinger mit den Provenzalen. Nicht nur von Seiten der Sitte gewinnen die unsern, sondern oft auch in Rücksicht der innigen Empfindung. In Süden, wenn ihr wollt, ist mehr Lustigkeit und Frechheit; hier mehr Liebe und Ehre, Bescheidenheit und Tugend, Verstand und Herz.[2]

To the extent that this is an attempt to distinguish the essential characteristics of the different types of literature it is a legitimate comparison. Nevertheless one is left with the impression that Herder is marking up

---

[1] Herder, xviii, pp. 135-6.   [2] *Ibid.*, xviii, p. 115.

points for each side and that he is more interested in the final score than he is in discovering the true nature of German and Provençal poetry. If this appears to be an unfair judgement let us turn to the conclusion of letter 106. Here Herder summarizes the qualities peculiar to the writings of the Italians, Spaniards, Frenchmen and Englishmen and compares them with the natural qualities of the Germans.

> Treue und Glauben, Unschuld der Sitten, Biederkeit und Einfalt – das seyn unsre Kastaliden! alles andre ist vergängliche Thorheit. Zur Italiänischen *acutezza*, zur Spanischen *grandezza*, zur Französischen *légèreté*, zum Brittischen *high-spirit* wird sich der Deutsche nie hinauf schwingen; was er aber ist und von jeher gewesen, davon ist seine eigne Geschichte eine durch Jahrhunderte erprobte Stimme der Wahrheit. Was alle Dichter singen, wohin sie wider Willen streben, was ihnen am meisten glückt, was bei denen, die sie lesen und hören, die grösseste Wirkung hervorbringt, das ist Charackter der Nation, wenn er auch als eine unbehauene Statue noch im Marmorblock daläge. Dies ist *Vernunft, reine Humanität, Einfalt, Treue* und *Wahrheit*. Wohl uns, dass uns dies sittliche Gefühl ward, dass dieser Charakter gleichsam von unsrer Sprache unabtrennlich ist, ja dass uns nichts gelingen will, wenn wir aus ihm schreiten.[1]

Italian, Spanish, French, and English writers are damned with faint praise. It is remarkable that Herder finds no more to say than this, in contrast to all the qualities which he heaps upon the Germans.

Fortunately, however, Herder demonstrates a much deeper and fairer appreciation of these other peoples in earlier letters. He has simply been carried away by his enthusiasm for the potentialities of the Germans and by his desire to encourage them. Indeed, he more or less excuses himself in the following letter when he says: "Keiner Nation dörfen wirs also verargen, wenn sie vor allen andern *ihre* Dichter liebt und sie gegen fremde nicht hingeben möchte; sie sind ja *ihre* Dichter."[2] Nevertheless there appears to be something inconsistent about Herder exercising his right as "der gebildete Mensch" in the same work in which he strongly advocates a relativistic approach to criticism. In letter 102 he makes some more detailed comparisons, rating Uz above Cowley, Hagedorn above Waller, Cronegk above Prior, Witthof above Akenside, and Gersten-

[1] Herder, xviii, pp. 133-4.   [2] *Ibid.*, xviii, p. 136.

berg above Otway and Waller. Sometimes it is not even clear that he is merely expressing a personal opinion, and his nationalism goes to absurd lengths. In comparing Haller with Pope he says:

> Was von Haller mit Pope verglichen werden kann, ist über Pope; was aus Pope's lebendiger Welt an feinen Satyren und Charakteren in feinem Reimgeklingel dasteht, würde Haller redlicher aufgestellt haben. Bewahre uns die Muse vor Dichtern, bei denen Verstand ohne Herz, oder Herz ohne Verstand ist. Zwei Popische Gedichte wünschte ich indessen meinem Vaterlande wohl eigen, seinen *Versuch über den Menschen und über die Kritik.* Ich habe nicht den mindesten Zweifel, dass wir beide besser, als Pope sie schrieb, zu ihrer Zeit bekommen werden. Unsres Hallers Gedichte sind ein Richtmaas der Sitten, so wie der Wissenschaft und Gendenkart.[1]

The last sentence of this passage is especially dubious in view of Herder's rejection of all such critical standards elsewhere in the same work. Perhaps Herder is only thinking in terms of a 'Richtmass' for other German writers, but the 'Unsres' indicates that he considers Haller's work to be exemplary for poets of other nations. The later letters contain many more invidious comparisons between English and German literature. On those occasions when it might be argued that Herder is simply describing the essential characteristics of each nation's literature his judgements seem to be arbitrary and unsound. Without offering any further explanation he asks the reader: "Nehmet eine ausgewählte Sammlung Deutscher Lieder und stellet sie der besten Englischen entgegen; an innerem Werthe, wohin wird die Waage sinken?"[2] The question is rhetorical; it is obvious that Herder ranks German poetry above English poetry in an important respect. 'Innerer Wert' is a phrase which can cover a lot of ground.

The section where Klopstock is placed alongside Milton provides the only fair and reasonable piece of comparative criticism in the latter part of the eighth collection. In fact Herder begins by wishing that the comparison between the two writers had never been made; but he proceeds to offer some interesting insights into the works of both men. He sums up the difference between them in the following manner:

---

[1] Herder, XVIII, p. 117.
[2] *Ibid.*, XVIII, p. 118.

Die Muse Miltons ist eine männliche Muse, wie sein Iambus; die Muse Klopstocks eine zärtere Muse, die in Erzählungen, Elegieen und Hymnen unsre ganze Seele, den Mittlepunkt ihrer Welt durchströmet. In Ansehung der Sprache hat Klopstock auf seine Nation mehr gewirkt, als Milton vielleicht auf die Seinige wirken konnte; wie er denn auch ungleich vielseitiger als der Britte über dieselbe gedacht hat.[1]

So far so good, but there follows a sentence which vitiates the whole piece. "Eine seiner Oden im Geschmack des Horaz ist nach dem Richtmaas der Alten mehr werth, als sämmtliche hochaufgethürmte Brittische Odengebäude."[2] To a genuine relativist this last remark would appear irrelevant. No doubt the British poets and Klopstock wrote their odes with Greek examples in mind, but their poetry should be judged on its own merits and not by any fixed standard. To dismiss all British odes out of hand simply because they do not closely resemble their Greek models is surely unwarranted according to the theories which Herder expounds only a few pages further on.

It is unfortunate that the nationalistic tendencies figure so strongly in the latter part of the eighth collection; they inevitably mingle with the conclusions which are drawn from both collections and in some cases render Herder's theoretical statements nugatory. On the other hand the last few letters illustrate effectively the extent to which Herder's interest in comparative literature was influenced by his nationalism. This conflict between the desire to stimulate and improve German writing and a theory of relativity which accords no nation a place of honour is much less evident in the seventh and the first half of the eighth collection. Those earlier letters contain much valuable material, and it is to them that we now turn.

Herder begins the seventh collection with the assumption that his readers are familiar with the classical authors of Greece and Rome. He sets out to examine the foundations of modern European literature and to see what sort of radical changes the advent of Christianity engendered in Europe. In the first *Fragment*, beginning in letter 81, he quotes a poem by Bishop Synesius from the year 410 to illustrate the change from Greek, 'Scherz und Freude' to a Platonic-Christian mixture of 'Andacht

[1] Herder, XVIII, p 118.   [2] *Ibid.*

und 'Weisheit'. Herder considers literature in the widest context possible; he realizes how closely it is tied to all social, religious and moral changes. As we have seen, Saint-Évremond also thought about the development of European literature in these terms. He was no less aware of the great changes wrought by the rise of Christianity, but Herder surpasses him by investigating more closely the precise nature of those changes. Despite his position as a pastor Herder recognizes certain disadvantages which Christianity brought with it. The national differences which he considers so important were temporarily obliterated. "Fortan war die Poesie keinem Volk, keinem Lande eigen, weil dieser Geist christlicher Hymnen, mit Zerstöhrung aller Nationalheiligthümer, die Völker insgesammt umfasste und glauben lehrte."[1]

A second result of the growth of Christianity was the separation of poetry and music, with the latter developing in its own right. John Brown had already discussed the implications of this development in his essay published in 1763. Another consequence was the linguistic mixture of the poetic genius of all races and the rise of a "Mönchssprache". "Im Innern konnte die Sprache eben so wenig rein bleiben, *da jetzt in Poesie und Rede der Genius fast aller Völker mit einander vermischt ward.*"[2] Finally there was the emphasis on the hereafter as opposed to the physical world, and the parallel development of Christian mysticism, which seriously impaired the whole structure of classical poetry. "Das Unendliche giebt kein Bild: denn es hat keinen Umriss; selten haben diesen auch die Poesieen, die das Unermessliche singen."[3] Just as Christian hands destroyed heathen statues and temples so Christian poetry stifled heathen poetry.

> Nicht nur wurden von den Christen jene Hymnen an Götter und Göttinnen, an Heroën und Genien als Werke der Ungläubigen oder der Abergläubigen angesehen; sondern und vorzüglich ward auch der Keim, der sie hervorgebracht hatte, die *dichtende oder spielende Einbildungskraft, die Lust und Fröhlichkeit des Volks an Nationalfesten* u.f. als eine Schule böser Dämonen verdammt, ja der *Nationalruhm selbst*, auf welchen jene Gesänge wirkten, als eine gefährlich-glänzende Sünde verachtet.[4]

[1] Herder, XVIII, p. 17.
[2] *Ibid.*, XVIII, p. 19.
[3] *Ibid.*, XVIII, p. 20.
[4] *Ibid.*, XVIII, p. 16.

The Hebrew psalms, which were the ultimate source for all Christian hymns, brought two supreme qualities with them. They were generally unoriginal and did not contain any new thoughts. "Selten sind es auch überraschend-feine und neue Empfindungen, mit denen sie uns etwa durchströmen; aufs neue und Feine ist in den Hymnen gar nicht gerechnet. Was ists denn, was uns rühret? Einfalt und Wahrheit."[1] It is interesting to note that at the end of the eighth collection Herder attributes these two qualities to the Germans, in contrast to the Italians, Spaniards, Frenchmen, Englishmen and other such allegedly Christian peoples.

Herder believes that the Germanic invaders who overran the Roman empire brought with them heroic songs about the deeds of their ancestors. "Diese Gesänge waren ja die ganze Wissenschaft und Geistesergötzung solcher barbarischen Völker, das Archiv ihres Ruhmes und Nachruhms."[2] Indeed, Herder declares that, in a coarser manner, these songs must have played as important a part in the lives of the people as Greek songs had done amongst the Greeks. He offers several reasons for the regrettable fact that these songs have not been preserved for posterity. "Die Veränderung und Mischung der Sprachen, bei den wandernden Völkern die Verschiedenheit des nordlichen und südlichen Klima, wohl aber am meisten der Fortgang der Sitten selbst hat uns dieser wahrscheinlich in rauhen Tönen besungenen Heldengestalten beraubet."[3] European poetry remained in a stagnant state until it received a stimulus from an outside source. The Moors who invaded Spain provided just such an impetus. The example of the Moors' "Galanterie" greatly affected the inhabitants of Spain and Southern France and was responsible for the refinement of the Provençal language. This in turn led to the burgeoning of Provençal poetry. Of the language Herder says: "Sie ist die Morgenröthe der *neueren* Europäischen Cultur und Dichtkunst."[4]

Letter 84 contains a brief historical and descriptive account of Provençal poetry. Herder provides no new information and readily acknowledges his indebtedness to several Italian and French writers,

---

[1] Herder, xviii, p. 15.   [2] *Ibid.*, xviii, p. 29.
[3] *Ibid.*, xviii, p. 30.   [4] *Ibid.*, xviii, p. 34.

prominent amongst whom is La Curne de Sainte-Palaye. Nor was Herder the first person to recognize the importance of Provençal poetry in the development of European literature. In France Pasquier had pointed out how much Dante and Petrarch, and consequently all other European nations, owed to the Provençal poets; and in England Rymer and Thomas Warton pursued the same subject further. Rymer had suggested that the origin of rhyme in European poetry could be traced back through the troubadours to the Arabs. In letter 84 Herder apparently dismisses the idea:

> Man hat über den Ursprung des Reims viel gestritten, und ihn bei Nordländern und Arabern, bei Mönchen, Griechen und Römern gesucht; mich dünkt mit unnöthiger Mühe. Man könnte über ihn das bekannte Kinderspiel mit dem Motto: "alles was reimen kann, reimt" spielen.[1]

He goes on to explain how the Provençal language, like Spanish, Portuguese, Italian, French and every other branch of the *lingua rustica Romana*, lacked the rhythm and "hohen lyrischen Wohlklang" of ancient Greek and Latin. The various different types of rhyme grew naturally from the special accentuation of Provençal:

> Jede Versart bekam ihre Strophe, d.i. ihren abgemessenen Perioden der Declamation in einer angewiesenen Ordnung und Art der Reime; in welcher *Wissenschaft* eben die *Kunst der Trobadoren* bestand. Und so haben wir die Gestalt der neuern Europäischen Dichtkunst, sofern sie sich von der Poesie der Alten unterscheidet, auf einmal vor uns. Sie war *Spiel*, eine *amusirende Hofverskunst in gereimten Formen*, weil der damaligen Sprache der Rhythmus und der damaligen Denkart der Zweck der Poesie der Alten fehlte.[2]

In letter 84 Herder seems to minimize the Arabic elements in Provençal poetry. He stresses the indigenous growth of the *gaya ciencia*, stimulated by the contact with the Arabs, but developing along its own lines. In the following letter he attributes much greater significance to the contribution of the Arabs. Even in the matter of rhyme he appears to have modified his opinion: "selbst die Prosodie der Provenzalen ward nach

---

[1] Herder, XVIII, pp. 35-6.   [2] *Ibid.*, XVIII, p. 37.

der blos accentuirten und declamirten arabischen Verskunst, in welcher der Reim unentbehrlich war, eingerichtet."[1] And Herder deems that the Arabic influence was just as great on the content as on the form of the troubadours' works. He admits that there were certain elements which the Europeans could not absorb. For example, "Mahomeds Lehre" was as alien to the latter as Homer and Greek mythology were to the Arabs. "Aber was sich aufnehmen liess, der Genius des Werks, die Arabische Denk- und Lebensweise; sie sind in den Versuchen der Provenzalen (diese mögen schlecht oder gut seyn), wie mir dünkt, unverkennbar."[2]

Herder proceeds to describe some of the peculiar qualities of the Arabs. Their poetical questions and answers, the reverence for their language and the poetry competitions; none of the European nations could match these things. "Die angrenzenden Christen, beschämt über ihre Rohheit, zuerst viellecht auch nur aus Nachamungssucht, folgten ihnen nach."[3] Arabic literature was imbued with three further qualities, which also passed into Provençal poetry and became an essential part of Christian literature – "Tapferkeit, Liebe und Andacht".[4] Finally Herder mentions one great gift to Europe which is equal in value to all of the Arabic "Reimgalanterie" – "jene Phantome Asiatischer Einbildungskraft nämlich, die vom Berge Kaf über Afrika und Spanien, über Palästina und die Tatarei zu uns gekommen sind."[5]

Letter 85 contains many acute observations and generalizations about the Arabs and their literature. It is, perhaps, ironic that, in spite of his later letter in which he speaks of the immense difficulties in attempting to characterize any nation as a whole, Herder excels in exactly this respect in his commentary on Arabic culture. Rymer and Warton had recognized that the Arabs contributed in some manner to European literature, but Herder far surpassed them in defining the exact nature of their gift. Yet his observations provide a greater paradox than this. Whenever Herder speaks of critical relativism he insists that each nation

[1] Herder, XVIII, p. 39.
[2] Ibid., XVIII, pp. 38-9.
[3] Ibid., XVIII, p. 39.
[4] Ibid.
[5] Ibid,, XVIII, p. 42.

has its own genius, but the qualities which the Europeans have apparently derived from the Arabs could scarcely be transmitted from one nation to another. Possibly the concepts of 'Tapferkeit', 'Liebe', and 'Andacht' could have passed from one people to the other, but surely "Einbildungskraft" is, in Herder's own terms, a native quality which cannot be artificially cultivated? The description of the manner in which the Europeans adopted various Arabic rhyme forms presents no problem, but the conflict between theory and practice becomes rather confusing when Herder discusses the transfer of Arabic ideas and attitudes.

The purpose of this careful examination of the origins and nature of Provençal poetry is revealed in letter 87. In this piece, which represents one of the best examples of his historical relativism, Herder attempts to show how certain European countries were influenced by the troubadours and adapted their work to suit the character of each nation. He begins by stating how widespread this influence was; even the English and German poets were affected. "Die Minnesinger sind unsre Provenzalen."[1] Subsequently, however, he devotes almost all of his attention to the nations of Southern Europe. Italian, Spanish and French poetry shared one thing in common; none of it could be adapted to the "Sylbemaasse" of the Greeks and Romans. Yet in true relativistic spirit Herder hastens to add: "nun müsste es wohl ein sehr barbarisches Ohr seyn, das nicht, zumal unter jenem Himmel, die Musik dieser Versarten fühlte."[2] He refers to the verse forms which were specially cultivated in Southern Europe, and were derived from Provençal poetry. There follows a general characterization of Italian poetry; in contrast to the ancients its essence is harmony and entertainment, in content and in form. "Eine Canzone oder Ode der Italiäner mit Pindar oder Horaz verglichen, hat, wie es uns Deutschen scheint, viel Declamation, viel prosaische, rednerische Schönheit".[3] In a few sentences Herder summarizes the peculiar qualities of Italian literature. "Die Poesie der Italiäner ist, was sie ihrem Urprunge nach seyn wollte, *Unterhaltung, accentuirte Conversation;* das ist ihr Standpunkt."[4] "Die ganze Dichtkunst Italiens

---

[1] Herder, XVIII, p. 47.   [2] *Ibid.*
[3] *Ibid.*, XVIII, p. 48.   [4] *Ibid.*

hat etwas sich Anneigendes, Freundliches und Holdes, dem die vielen weiblichen Reime angenehm zu Hülfe kommen, und es der Seele sanft einschmeicheln."[1]

Between these general statements Herder mentions various Italian authors whose works seem to support his thesis. He is, however, working from the general to the particular and he does not offer any detailed analyses of individual writers. In the comments about Italian pastoral poetry, which provide as clear an example of historical relativism as any to be found in Herder's work, he makes one central point. The attitude towards love in such works, which is so alien to German readers, must not be judged by inappropriate standards:

> nimmt man indessen das Local der Italiäner, die Zeit, in welcher diese Dichter lebten, die einmal getroffene Arabisch-Provenzalische Convention, *über die Liebe in Reimen zu conversiren*, auch viele kleine Umstände der damaligen Lebensweise zusammen: so werden uns diese musikalische Liebes-Conversationen nicht nur erklärlich, sondern beinahe natürlich erscheinen.[2]

Although Herder refers to Tasso's *Aminta* and Guarini's *Pastor fido* he is more concerned with a general phenomenon than with particular works. Earlier we noted an apparent logical contradiction in Herder's theories: either one can understand the writers of a country by examining the language, environment and people or vice versa, but it is difficult to proceed in both directions at the same time. Here in practice, in letter 87, Herder firmly takes the first approach. The discussion of Metastasio's work illustrates this point clearly. After he has established the general character of Italian poetry Herder declares that it reached the highest natural form of expression in the opera. There follows a short description of Metastasio's operas in general, without any allusions to specific works, and an account of the development of Italian 'Melodrama' "seit es in rauhen Provenzalischen Canzonen nach Italien gekommen und von umherziehenden Ministrels mit einer Art theatralischen Vorstellung verbunden hie und da gespielt war!"[3] Although Herder admires Metastasio he sees him more as a representative of Italian culture than as

---

[1] *Ibid.*, XVIII, p. 49.   [2] *Ibid.*, XVIII, p. 50.   [3] *Ibid.*

an individual. "Metastasio kam, und setzte der ganzen Gattung den Kranz auf."[1]

In the next section of this *Fragment* Herder subjects French literature to similar scrutiny. Again he selects those features which all writers have in common. "Der Zweig der Provenzalischen Dichtkunst, der sich in *Frankreich* verbreitete, trug andere Früchte. Die Französische Sprache, die lange nicht so sangbar war, als die Italiänische, hatte desto mehrere Lust zu *erzählen*, und zu *repräsentiren*."[2] In the cursory survey of French literary history which follows the emphasis is upon "erzählen" and "repräsentiren". This leads to some distortion. Perhaps it can be fairly argued that Villon, Rabelais and Marot were primarily notable for their ability to recount a story. Whether this is true of Montaigne, Voltaire and Diderot is doubtful, but still plausible. Few literary historians, however, would agree with Herder's statement about the age of Louis xiv. "Im goldnen Zeitalter Ludwigs endlich war ein Erzähler, *La Fontaine*, wohl das eigenthümlichste Genie, dessen Grazie nicht veralten wird, so lange die französische Sprache dauret."[3] Even if one were to concede the position of honour to La Fontaine it is surely necessary to mention the claims of other great writers of the period, such as Racine, Corneille and Molière. Yet Herder does not do so. Nor does he consider any of the great dramatists when he discusses the French proclivity for "Repräsentation".

We observed a distinct anti-French bias in some of Herder's earlier works and traces of this feeling remain in the *Humanitätsbriefe*. He does not roundly condemn the French passion for representation, but he gives certain hints of his disapproval:

> Dagegen was *Repräsentation* nicht leistet, was manchmal z.B. im Trauerspiele sie sogar nicht wünschet und gern verbirgt, die tiefere Wahrheit und Natur der Leidenschaften dem französischen Theater, verglichen mit dem Griechischen und Englischen, oft fremd blieb. Sowohl der *Heroismus* als die *Liebe* erscheinen in der französischen Theaterkunst, (von vortreflichen Ausnahmen ist hier nicht die Rede) nach dem Gesetz einer National-Convention *repräsentiret*.[4]

---

[1] Herder, xviii, p. 51.
[2] *Ibid.*, xviii, p. 52.
[3] *Ibid.*, xviii, p. 53.
[4] *Ibid.*, xviii, p. 54.

One wonders exactly what "excellent exceptions" he had in mind. It is perhaps legitimate to describe the essential characteristics of French literature by pointing out the elements which it lacks in comparison with that of other nations; but this accords ill with Herder's own recommendation at the end of the eighth collection – "jede Blume an ihrem Ort zu lassen." One might be inclined to regard this as a trivial point if Herder had taken a similar line of approach in the first part of the letter, dealing with Italian literature. Such is not the case. He draws comparisons between Italian and Greek literature and is always ready with excuses for the former. After explaining how Italian rhymed verse constantly detains the reader, whereas classical hexameters flow along without interruption, he closes the matter with the comment: "So könnte man mehr vergleichen; wozu aber die Vergleichung, wenn sie den Genuss störet?"[1]

The aim of all Italian poets, according to Herder, is to please and entertain, but only a native Italian can judge whether they are successful in their undertaking. "Ob diesen Zweck jede dieser Poësieen erreicht habe? darüber kann kein Ausländer entscheiden; indessen scheinets."[2] Herder also defends Metastasio for his somewhat light-hearted attitude towards the theatre. "Wenn also Metastasio in jedem seiner Stücke einen zierlichen Porcellanthurm mit klingenden Silberglöckchen erbauen wollte: so sollte und konnte dieser kein griechisches Odeum werden."[3] He gives the Italians the benefit of the doubt and finds that it is his duty to explain and defend them rather than to criticize. When he turns to French literature he is not content to allow Frenchmen to decide whether their "Repräsentation" is a worthy purpose; and although he does not offer any proof that it is more frivolous than the spirit of Metastasio's operas, he adopts a critical posture in regard to "Repräsentiren."

The impression of prejudice against the French is strengthened by the remarks about the Spaniards, which conclude the letter. Herder lays stress on the positive qualities of Spanish literature. In contrast to the situation in Italy and France Spanish culture was not borrowed from

[1] Herder, XVIII, p. 48.   [2] Ibid., XVIII, p. 49.   [3] Ibid., XVIII, p. 51.

that of Provence. They grew up alongside each other and more or less in competition. The long occupation of Spain by the Arabs helped to stimulate the special genius of Spanish writing: "es ist die Idee eines *christlichen* Ritterthums, den Heiden und Ungläubigen entgegen."[1] Their language stands somewhere between Italian and Latin, and the dignity of the latter lends it a certain "Wohlklang". The Spaniards have exceptionally "scharfsinnige Sprüche" and "ihre Erzählungen, Theaterstücke und Romane sind voll Verwickelungen, voll Tiefsinnes und bei vielem Befremdenden voll feiner und grosser Gedanken."[2] The closing remark shows the same sympathetic attitude towards the Spaniards as was shown towards the Italians. "Sie sind veredelte Araber; auch ihre Thorheit hat etwas Andächtiges und Erhabnes."[3] In this final section Herder carries his method of examining the literature of a nation through the character of the people and the language to the extreme; he does not mention a single Spanish writer.

The seventh collection closes with a summary of the condition of European poetry in the period which followed the introduction and spreading of Provençal poetry. Herder sees two great hindrances to the advancement of literature; the currency of vulgar Latin, a decadent language which was unfortunately mixed with the various native tongues, and the "Sitten dieser Nationen selbst, im mittleren Zeitalter."[4] The people were filled with a war-like spirit and Herder selects as the key words "Abentheuer" and "Roman". In their desire for adventure stories they displayed extreme gullibility which more or less precluded the possibility of refinement. The Arabs had provided three important ingredients for any improvement – "Liebe, Tapferkeit und Andacht" – but these three ideals had also been slightly tarnished by the Europeans. Love was not always that admirable emotion of the "Minnelieder". At many of the courts the sort of gallantry which is described in the *Decameron* was quite common. Apart from their duty to their equals, their overlords, their ladies and the church the knights considered that they could do anything that they wished to do. Consequently the poetry of

---

[1] Herder, xviii, p. 56. [2] *Ibid.*
[3] *Ibid.*, xviii, p. 56. [4] *Ibid.*, xviii, p. 59.

the period was either filled with hollow and dreary passages about the demands and honour of knighthood, or it condoned the brutal abuse of power in the name of knighthood. "Andacht" tended to turn into mere "Feierlichkeit" and thus become quite tedious.

All these faults stemmed from the decay of religion and morals. The "fröhliche Wissenschaft" of the courts did not help matters as the decadence spread to all classes. Herder declares that there are only two qualities which can be of lasting value and beauty: "So gewiss ists, dass nichts bleibend schön seyn kann, als das Wahre und Gute."[1] The presence or lack of these in poetry must eventually become evident. Nevertheless the Europeans did add something to the qualities which the Arabs had given to them. Mariolatry and the general reverence for womanhood went beyond anything the Greeks had known, and the ideals of knighthood were by no means all bad. If such rules as that which called for the protection of the weak were properly observed Christian knighthood held even wider possibilities than the Greek ideal of bravery. One danger for mediaeval poetry was the growth of scientific knowledge, which threatened to smother it in scholastic details. It was, however, also possible to make good use of the extra knowledge; "nicht vergebens hat der Vater der neueren Dichtkunst, Dante, mit einem Werk begonnen, das eine Art von Encyklopedie des menschlichen Wissens über Himmel und Erde enthält."[2] Perhaps the best praise which Herder could bestow upon mediaeval poetry is the assertion that it was moving unmistakably towards that "Grazie der Grazien" 'carita'.

The eighth collection opens with the claim that true progress in European culture did not begin until the Renaissance. The poetry of the middle ages didn't lack subject matter, good will, purpose or ideals, but there was no "Geschmack, innere Norm und Regel."[3] Only the ancients could provide that. Herder goes on to describe the arrival of Greek scholars in Italy and he stresses the inspiration which these men gave to artists such as Raphael. Europe was raised out of the dusk of "Ritter-romane". "Das Licht der Alten ists, das die Schatten verjagt und die Dämmerung aufgeklärt hat; mit ihnen haben wir empfangen, was allein

---

[1] Herder, XVIII, p. 61.   [2] Ibid., XVIII, p. 65.   [3] Ibid., XVIII, p. 72.

den Geschmack sichert, *Verhältniss, Regel, Richtmaas, Form der Gestalten im weiten Reiche der Natur und Kunst, ja der gesammten Menschheit.*[1] The letter continues in this vein; the mediaeval view of love, the exaggerated "Ritterwürde" and "Andacht" are compared unfavourably with the simplicity and truth of the ancients. Finally Herder declares that there is no genuine modern European criticism: one can only speak of the palingenesis of Greek and Roman criticism, which stimulated the search for better taste in Europe.

At this stage it appears as if Herder has suddenly abandoned his belief in relativity and become as keen an advocate of classicism as Gottsched ever was. The next letter, however, quickly dispels this impression by providing an almost complete rebuttal of the arguments in letter 91. There were great men who have lived since that time, and who have had practically no knowledge of classical authors. One needs only to think of Dante and Shakespeare. "Die grössten Erfindungen sind in den Zeiten gemacht, die wir *barbarische, rohe* Zeiten nennen; vielleicht haben in ihnen auch die grössesten Männer gelebet."[2] Herder reaffirms his support for relativity by citing the example of some of Europe's greatest writers:

> Woher nahmen *Ariost* und die ihm vorgingen, woher *Spenser, Shakespeare* und zwar in seinen rührendsten Stücken Form und Inhalt? Nicht aus den Alten, sondern aus der *Denkart des Volks und seinem Geschmack in ihren und den mittleren Zeiten.*[3]

Despite a great increase in the quantity and quality of classical scholarship since Shakespeare's time no serious rival has appeared. A knowledge of the classics is no substitute for original creative ability, as witness the efforts of Trissino, Gravina, Maffei and Cowley.

Basically these arguments are familiar; some of the earliest critics whom we have discussed, Daniel in England and Ogier in France, occupied almost the same ground in defence of relativism. In letter 93 Herder tries to provide a synthesis of the views expressed in the previous two letters. Every nation possesses some talent, but unfavourable conditions may prevent it from fructifying. If the language of a country is not

---

[1] Herder, XVIII, pp. 73-4.   [2] *Ibid.*, XVIII, p. 77.   [3] *Ibid.*, XVIII, p. 78.

highly developed its poets will not have a proper instrument and will thus be severely handicapped. Although the Greeks do not enjoy a monopoly in the arts they occupy a uniquely favourable position. "Wem gab nun die Natur das eigentliche *Kunsttalent* in grösserm Maasse, als den Griechen? Auf der ganzen Erde keinem Volke wie ihnen."[1] Consequently they may serve as guides to other nations. "*Aufmunterung, Ordnung, Verbesserung* ist ihr einziger Zweck; man darf also von ihnen nicht mehr fodern, als sie zu leisten vermögen. Sie wollen Kräfte wecken, aber nicht geben; sie sind Vorbilder, keine Schöpfer."[2]

Earlier in this chapter we observed that there appeared to be some confusion in Herder's mind about the value of studying foreign literature. Here he does not appear to be in any doubt about the benefits to be gained from studying the writers of antiquity. He repeats the lesson in letter 94: "Einfalt also und Würde, Bedeutsamkeit und Wohlordnung haben wir von den Alten zu lernen, um unsrer Denkart und Sprache im Kleinsten und Grössesten eine solche Gestalt zu geben."[3] In the following letter, however, Herder raises again some of the doubts which he had expressed in earlier essays. He considers the advantages and disadvantages which the invention of printing has given to Europe and uses many of the arguments contained in *Über die Wirkung der Dichtkunst* and in *Ursachen des gesunknen Geschmacks.* A vast amount of information became available and for the few people who could sort and absorb it all this was most helpful. Yet for the majority it merely brought confusion: they could hardly avoid becoming bookworms "und zuletzt selbst in Person *gedruckte Buchstaben*". "Und wenn dir jetzt täglich nur zehn Tages – und Zeitschriften zufliegen und in jedem nur fünf Stimmen zutönen; wo hast du am Ende deinen Kopf? wo behältst du Zeit zu eignem Nachdenken und zu Geschäften?"[4]

Herder asks himself whether Homer, Sophocles, Horace, Dante, Petrarch, Shakespeare or Milton would have written their great works in such a world of books and reading. The answer is "schwerlich". One might object that the last five writers named were demonstrably well-

[1] *Ibid.,* xviii, p. 81.   [2] *Ibid.,* xviii, p. 82.
[3] *Ibid.,* xviii, p. 85.   [4] *Ibid.,* xviii, p. 91.

read men, but the point is still well taken. The eighteenth century had seen a considerable growth in all sorts of printed material. Herder offers an explanation of the process:

> Denn unverkennbar ists, dass jemehr durch die Buchdruckerei die Werke aller Nationen allen gemein wurden, der ruhige Gang eigenthümlicher Composition grossentheils aufgehört hat. Wer fürs Publicum schreibt, schreibt selten mehr ganz *für sich* als den innersten Richter; daher Pascal und Rousseau unter so vielen Autoren so wenige Menschen fanden.[1]

Clearly Herder is concerned principally with the problem of the creative writer, and, as we have observed, the main reason why he studied comparative literature was to stimulate the growth of German letters. Nevertheless the literary critic who concerns himself with literature from all nations also runs the risk of being swamped by the mass of material. One could well argue that these observations have even more relevance today than they had in 1796.

We return, in letter 97, to the consideration of the development of European literature. Herder claims that revolutions in taste always follow great events and he takes as an example the period of the Reformation. The discovery of the new world and new ideas in finance and the sciences sent the poetry of the middle ages to its grave. "Die Reformation selbst ist weniger eines heroischen Lob – als eines philosophischen Lehrgedichts fähig."[2] At this point a great division took place amongst the peoples of Europe. Italy, Spain and other Catholic lands held fast to their old forms of poetry: the longer they had enjoyed "guten Geschmack" and the more deeply rooted it was in their country "je grössere Vorbilder sie besassen: desto vester hingen sie an ihren Stanzen und Reimen."[3] Yet the adherence to old forms did not prevent them from introducing new ideas into their works.

On the other hand "eine Freimüthigkeit im Denken" spread throughout the Protestant countries and their poetry took on a more philosophical character. "Unvermerkt also nahm die Poesie der neuen Glaubens-Verwandten eine philosophische Hülle um sich, die der Sinnlichkeit

---

[1] *Ibid.*   [2] *Ibid.*, xviii, p. 95.   [3] *Ibid.*, xviii, p. 96.

vielleicht schadete, dem menschlichen Geist aber nothwendig war."[1] Thus an Italian finds nothing lyrical in most English odes, because melody and harmony are lacking. Herder also mentions Sir William Jones' assertion that there is nothing poetical about Milton's works according to oriental standards. He adds the comment: "Vielen Deutschen Dichtern würde es nicht besser ergehen: denn offenbar sind die meisten *nur durch Reflexion* Dichter."[2]

In the seventh collection Herder concentrated his attention upon Italian, French and Spanish poetry and tended to neglect the English. In this and the succeeding letter he compensates fully for the previous lack of attention: he cites examples from English literature to illustrate many of his general observations. Describing the effect of the Reformation on subsequent literature he says: "Seit der Reformation und dem hellaufgegangnen Licht der Wissenschaften gelangen also *keine persönlichen Heldengedichte* mehr, mit dem Wunderbaren der alten Zeit bekleidet."[3] Ariosto was able to incorporate fairly tales in his poetry purely for the purpose of entertainment without any demand on serious belief. Wieland could do the same in *Oberon;* but Tasso was unsuccessful when he tried to mix such "Mährchen" with a religion in which he believed. Likewise Milton's work suffers from the imposition of a religious system. For the same reason, namely the want of credibility, there have been no successful historical epics in modern times. The Elizabethan age in England was celebrated only in sonnets or allegories, and that of Cromwell and the Restoration only in odes. The conflict between history and poetry vitiates Chapelain's *Jeanne d'Arc* and Voltaire's *Henriade.* The same situation has prevailed in Germany: the mixture of fable and truth is no longer acceptable in Europe after the Reformation.

The emphasis suddenly switches to English literature as Herder explains that the pure muse will not tolerate an excess of bitterness. Thus personal satires are doomed to oblivion. He admits that Butler's *Hudibras* is instructive and full of wit, but who would not wish, he asks, that the author had put his talent to a nobler use? He also praises Swift's abilities highly and regrets that he indulged himself so freely in satire: Herder

[1] Herder, XVIII, p. 96.   [2] *Ibid.*   [3] *Ibid.,* XVIII, p. 97.

recognizes this, however, as a common fault of the English. "Alles, was die Engländer *Humour* nennen, ist Uebertreibung; ein verzeihlicher Fehler der Natur, der hie und da zur Schönheit werden kann, nur aber zu einer National- und Zeitschönheit."[1] To complete the letter Herder refers to three further general flaws in European poetry. Most attempts at detailed description only succeed in blurring the picture; the poet smothers the object which he is trying to depict in a welter of imagery. "So manche poetische *Landbeschreibung* der Engländer steht da, dass sie uns mit sehenden Augen blind mache; so manche andre, dass wir bei *Umschreibungen bekannter Gegenstände oder Begriffe* gar nichts denken sollen."[2] The last two weaknesses are not specifically connected with English poetry. Most metaphysical poems of all nations have been superceded by the discovery of a new system of philosophy, and finally "das *Unmoralische* des Dichters" will succumb to "das *reine Menschengefühl*".

The examination of the essential changes which occurred approximately at the time of the Reformation, with special reference to English literature, continues in letter 98. Herder has already established the true nature of English poetry – "eine *denkende* ist die Brittische Muse"[3] – and he now explains the basic distinction between "*Poesie aus Reflexion*" and "die *reine Fabelpoesie*". The minstrel of the middle ages only wished to present some remarkable event to his audience; he made no attempt to draw attention to himself. Such was the case with Chaucer, Spenser and other contemporaries. "Der erste in seinen *Canterbury-Tales* erzählt völlig noch als ein *Troubadour;* er hat eine Reihe ergötzender Mährchen zu seinem Zweck der Zeitkürzung und Lehre, charakteristisch für alle Stände und Personen, die er erzählend einführt, geordnet."[4] There is an absolute minimum of intrusion by the author. The Reformation brought to an end the "Ritter-und Feenwelt" with its simple manner of presentation. "Die Dichter waren nicht mehr einfache Sänger fremder Begebenheiten, sondern *gelehrte Männer*, die uns das Gebäude ihres eignen Kopfs zur Schau bringen wollten, indem sie dasselbe wohl durchdacht niederschreiben, damit wirs lesen."[5]

[1] Herder, XVIII, p. 99.
[2] *Ibid.*
[3] *Ibid.*, XVIII, p. 97.
[4] *Ibid.*, XVIII, p. 100.
[5] *Ibid.*, XVIII, p. 101.

Herder believes that Shakespeare represents the watershed between the two types of poet. He explains how Shakespeare manages to combine the fairy-tale world of the ministrel with a deep philosophical understanding which encompasses all classes of men, without imposing himself forcefully upon his audience. Modern English poetry really begins with Milton, one of the most reflective of all poets. Language stood at his command and he had a high purpose to fulfill. "Nicht wollte er etwa blos Zeitkürzend vergnügen, sondern belehrend erbauen, und seine Encyklopädie von Wahrheiten in einer heiligen Sprache veststellend verewigen."[1] Herder describes how Milton used iambic metre with great skill, in a noble but sometimes monotonous manner. Every phrase, cadence and image was carefully thought out, and none of his successors could equal him in his mastery of the language. English is on the whole a rather monosyllabic tongue, but Milton manages to ring the changes from monosyllabic to polysyllabic words most adeptly and avoids the barbarous dissonance displayed by the lesser writers of his day.

After giving this outline of Milton's achievement Herder turns his attention to some of these less important poets. He concedes that Cowley was well steeped in classical philosophy and literature, and that he had a fine feeling for the beauty of nature. In spite of these advantages, however, he produced infelicitous Pindaric odes. Although they contain many fine thoughts they are quite spoiled by shafts of wit, which are out of place. Herder mentions various other writers who tried their hand in the same genre with no greater success. "Sie ist und bleibt ein gothisches Gebäude, unzusammenhängend und unübersehbar in ihren Theilen, übertrieben in Bildern, mit Zierrath überladen, in der Abwechslung des Rhythmus ungleich und unharmonisch."[2] Writers such as Waller, Prior and Littleton filled their works with gallantry and fashionable poetry and consequently their fame was quite transitory. "Spielender Witz" disappeared with the court of Charles II and the British muse reverted to its true role as a thoughtful muse. "Dryden voran, Pope nach ihm zeigten, worinn die Poesie der Neueren am natürlichsten bestehe, nämlich in *versificirtem gesundem Verstande*."[3]

---

[1] Herder, XVIII, p. 102.   [2] *Ibid.*, XVIII, p. 104.   [3] *Ibid.*, XVIII, p. 105.

Herder gives Pope credit for doing in English what Metastasio had done in the much more melodic Italian language: he reduced all sorts of philosophical principles and wisdom to short, pithy rhymed couplets. Indeed, he suggests that Pope's work may be regarded as "eine gereimte Blüthensammlung aller Moral, auch vieler Weltkänntniss und Weltklugheit." "Höher hinaus aber reichte sein Genius nicht."[1] His appraisal of Pope coincides quite closely with the opinion of Joseph Warton, but it is perfectly reasonable to suppose that Herder arrived independently at these conclusions. Taking into account, for example, Herder's previous critical pronouncements one might expect him to be just as disturbed as Warton was by the mixture of modern and classical elements in Pope's work. Herder's objection to the "Geklingel von Reimen" in Pope's translation of Homer is perfectly in keeping with his criticism, almost thirty years earlier, of the metre which Denis chose for his translation of Ossian.

The letter closes with some brief remarks about Young and Thomson, emphasizing the philosophical nature of their work in order to show how English poetry has been "eine *reflectirende* Poesie" since Milton's time. Herder adopts a surprisingly critical attitude towards Young: "Mich wundert, dass man *Young* je für einen tiefsinnigen Dichter gehalten hat; ein äusserst witziger, parenthyrsisch-beredter, nach Originalität aufstrebender Dichter ist er auf allen Seiten. Reich an Gedanken und Bildern, wusste er in ihnen weder Ziel noch Maas."[2] As we have seen in an earlier chapter, in his youth Herder was most enthusiatic about Young's works, and although he may not have actually used the word "tiefsinnig" he certainly praised them highly on many occasions. Indeed, he appears to have changed his mind again after writing the *Humanitätsbriefe*. In *Adrastea* (1801) we find the following comment: "*Youngs* Nachtgedanken endlich sind das *Non plus ultra* sinnreicher, witziger, erhabner, frommer Gedanken, glänzend wie das nächtliche Firmament; wer mag sie ordnen und zählen?"[3]

Herder has left until the last the richest field for English literary talent – "*die einkleidende Prose*". By this he means the novel, which he discusses in

---

[1] *Ibid.*   [2] *Ibid.*, XVIII, p. 107.   [3] *Ibid.*, XVIII, p. 236.

letter 99. Somewhat unexpectedly he selects Shakespeare as the founding father of this genre; the reason for this choice is simple:

> Er hatte Charaktere und Leidenschaften so tief aus dem Grunde geschildert, die verschiedenen Stände, Alter, Geschlechter, und Situationen der Menschen so wesentlich und energisch gezeichnet, dass ihm der Wechsel des Ortes und der Zeit, Griechenland, Rom, Sicilien und Böhmen durchaus keine Hindernisse in den Weg legten, und er mit der leichtesten Hand dort und hier hervorgerufen hatte, was er wollte.[1]

In each of his plays there lies a philosophical novel and altogether these set the tone for the development of the novel in England after the disappearance of "Ritter- und Liebesgeschichten" such as are contained in Sir Philip Sidney's *Arcadia*.

To explain the process Herder introduces sociological and historical factors. Since the third estate had acquired a voice in politics at an early date each class had its own character and did not merely try to imitate the one above. English "*humour*" derives from this "Freimüthigkeit" and the desire of each class to display independent characteristics. "Wie aber der Italiäner seinen Capricci, der Franzose seiner Gaskonade freien Lauf lässt, so gab der Engländer seinem trägeren *humour* nach; ein grosses Feld für Komödien und Romane –"[2] In addition the journals and weekly magazines exercised a considerable influence on the English style of writing: in particular Herder recognizes the debt which the English novel owes to Swift (for his "Genauigkeit" and "Proprietät") and to Addison and Steele (for their "goldne *Mittelmässigkeit*"). Finally he mentions "die drei glücklichen Romanhelden" Fielding, Richardson and Sterne, but he does not enter into any analyses of their works. He simply stresses the great range and possibilities of the genre and suggests that some of the greatest classical authors, including Homer, Herodotus, Xenophon, Plato and Lucian wrote "Romane in ihrer Art".

At this point Herder's nationalistic feelings assert themselves. The rest of the eighth collection is devoted to a discussion of the bright future for German literature and to the comparisons between German and English

---

[1] *Ibid.*, XVIII, p. 107.   [2] *Ibid.*, XVIII, p. 108.

writers, which we considered earlier in this chapter. The mixture of relativism and nationalism in these last letters brings nothing essentially new to comparative literature. Perhaps no one had expressed such a fervent admiration for German literature and the German people before, but we have observed the national prejudice and the principle of relativity in many earlier critics. What, then, is Herder's contribution to comparative literature, as seen through the seventh and the first part of the eighth collection of the *Humanitätsbriefe*?

The easiest manner in which to begin an answer to this question is to state what is not new in Herder's work. There is comparatively little factual information about German or foreign literature and in those letters which do contain historical accounts Herder relies upon earlier published sources. For instance, he tells us practially nothing about Provençal poetry which we could not find in the works of Pasquier, La Curne de Sainte-Palaye, Rymer and Warton. He provides us with opinions rather than facts and generally expresses his views in terms of nations and peoples rather than examining and comparing individual authors. His purpose is to show how the character of a people is reflected in its literature. Saint-Évremond and Muralt had tried to demonstrate the connection between literature and society long before Herder was born: and Saint-Évremond had even anticipated Herder's conclusion about the philosophical nature of English poetry.[1]

What distinguishes Herder from all previous writers is the range and depth of his work. He did not bring any great new theory to the study of comparative literature, but simply followed through schemes suggested by earlier critics. Saint-Évremond, Perrault and Villate, for example, had recognized the importance of the growth of Christianity in the history of European literature, but they left it to Herder to investigate the subject thoroughly. His survey of the role of Provençal poetry in Europe is more comprehensive than any single previous account, as he draws his information from several different sources and adds some ideas of his own. His study of the essential nature and development of the various national literatures of modern Europe is more

[1] Saint-Évremond, *op. cit.*, II, p. 384.

extensive than that of any of his predecessors, with the possible exception of Morhof.

In one respect, therefore, it is, perhaps, slightly misleading to speak of Herder as a pioneer in the field of comparative literature. Louis Betz made this point clear in his brief outline of the development of the discipline:

> Wohl waren die Lessing, Herder, Schiller, Tieck, die beiden Schlegel – besonders aber Herder, Meister der vergleichenden litterarischen Kritik, wohl standen sie auf ungleich höherer Warte, wohl war ihr Urteil viel reifer, als das der Perrault, St. Evremond und Fontenelle; aber sie kamen dafür auch 100 Jahre später.[1]

As a translator and propagator of foreign literature through the *Volkslieder* and *Der Cid*, however, Herder merits the title of pioneer. Furthermore, although many of his ideas about comparative literature were not original, the phrase "auf ungleich höherer Warte" is pertinent. Not only did he combine the ideas of many earlier critics, but he generated more enthusiasm for the subject than any previous writer. No matter how derivative one may prove his ideas to be, his influence has been so great that he must always remain an important figure in the history of comparative literature.

[1] Louis Betz, "Litteraturvergleichung," *Das litterarische Echo*, III (1901), p. 659.

CHAPTER VI

CONCLUSION

Any critic who claims to offer a complete account of Herder's work without referring to his contribution to comparative literature clearly does Herder an unjustice. Likewise, no survey of the history of comparative literature is complete without recognition of Herder's role. His work as a translator and the collection of *Volkslieder* alone should assure him a place of honour. It is, however, something of an exaggeration to call him the founding father of modern comparative literature. Indeed, bearing in mind the sharp disagreement amongst comparatists about the exact nature of their discipline, a matter which we discussed at the beginning of this study, it is highly improbable that any writer could reasonably have such a claim made on his behalf.

For those who believe only in the comparison of actual texts Pasquier and Rymer must appear to be of great importance; and presumably they would value Lessing's detailed analysis of French, English, Italian and Spanish plays more highly than any of Herder's generalizations about various national characteristics. According to the looser definition of comparative literature, which we accepted, Herder was certainly not the first modern comparatist. Many critics before him, in France, England and Germany, interested themselves in the literature of their European neighbours.

The purpose of this study was not to provide a complete early history of comparative literature; it was rather to establish to what extent Herder's contribution to the field was original. We have seen how certain writers in different countries preceded him in making a general survey of European literature. Some of these pieces are not very extensive in

141

scope and consequently pale into insignificance when placed beside the *Humanitätsbriefe*. Morhof's work, however, represents a genuine milestone. The *Unterricht von der Teutschen Sprache und Poesie* alone would be a sufficient cause to deny Herder the position of the earliest modern comparatist. Certainly Morhof deserves more attention and credit than he has hitherto been given.

Of the English critics the work of Blair, Hayley and Beattie has been unduly neglected, although it is probably not so important as that of Morhof. And the French contributions of Saint-Évremond and Voltaire have been seriously underestimated. The interest of the former in the connection between national character and literature represents an important new branch of comparative literary studies. His knowledge of foreign literature was fairly limited and so he did not probe very deeply; but he was the first to tread this path. Voltaire demonstrated, in the earlier part of his career, a considerable interest in and knowledge of the drama and the epic outside his native country.

Herder himself complained that the Germans had occupied themselves too assiduously with foreign literature. Although on occasion he entertained serious doubts, the main purpose of his criticism was not to stifle the study of comparative literature in Germany, but rather to put an end to servile imitation of foreign models. Indeed, one can hardly classify mere imitation of foreign literature as comparative literature. Herder's concern about the imitative nature of German literature was clearly justified, but he was by no means the first writer to consider this problem. Gottsched's opponents had taken strong objection to his attitude towards French classicism and several writers had attempted to show how Germany had a greater affinity with England than with France.

At first sight it may appear as if these critics were merely trying to substitute one form of imitation for another and were thus approaching no nearer to true comparative literature; on closer inspection it will be seen that such a view is untenable. Writers such as Schlegel and Lessing were inevitably led to examine the comparative merits of French and English literature; one of the best known of Lessing's critical writings, the seventeenth *Litteraturbrief*, provides ample proof of this fact. The brief analysis of the essential differences between Corneille and Shakespeare must definitely be considered as a study in comparative literature. The German critics of the first half of the eighteenth century did not regard English literature solely as a replacement for French literature. They began to show an interest in the intrinsic merits of certain English authors. With his comparison of Gryphius and Shakespeare Schlegel initiated the serious study and appreciation of Shakespeare in Germany. Bodmer demonstrated a genuine interest in the work of Milton. In his observations about the establishment of a national theatre in Denmark Schlegel even preceded Herder in focusing attention on the relationship between the character of a people and their literature. Bodmer and Breitinger had made a modest start in this direction with their comparison of the treatment of Queen Sophonisbe by Corneille, Trissino, Lee and Lohenstein. Lessing carried this method much farther with his detailed analyses of French, English, Spanish and Italian plays upon the same theme.

The contents of the journals and reviews of the 1750's and 1760's give evidence of the tremendous upsurge of interest in foreign literature. The work of such men as Meinhard and Bertram contributed to the generally cosmopolitan literary atmostphere which prevailed when Herder appeared upon the scene. Herder's first important work, the first collection of *Fragmente*, appeared almost simultaneously with Gerstenberg's *Briefe über Merkwürdigkeiten der Litteratur*, a work which displays a wide knowledge of European literature and deals with many of the topics with which Herder later concerned himself. Herder admitted his debt to Gerstenberg for ideas about Shakespeare.

According to our original definition of comparative literature it cannot be reasonably maintained that Herder was the first modern comparatist. Nor can one seriously argue that he was the first comparatist who was aware of what he was doing and who followed a definite method. There is no reason to suppose that Morhof did not realize the implications of his undertaking and the *Unterricht* is just as systematically organized as the *Humanitätsbriefe*. Certainly, Herder investigated the differences between the various national literatures more thoroughly than Morhof, but basically both writers offered a systematic survey of European literature. Indeed, it is possible that Morhof wrote more in the spirit of modern comparative literature than Herder did. The spirit of nationalism is much less evident in the *Unterricht* than in the *Humanitätsbriefe*. In all of Herder's works which are concerned with comparative literature, from the *Fragmente* through the *Volkslieder* and prize essays right down to the *Humanitätsbriefe*, a nationalistic tone predominates.

The main purpose of collecting and translating the folksongs from various nations was to inspire some German writer to gather together the German heritage, and thus provide a rich source for the development of their national literature. Similarly the object of the survey of European literature in the *Humanitätsbriefe* was to stimulate the Germans in the hope that they would try to emulate the achievements of other European nations. It is true that most of the comparatists whom we have considered in this study displayed certain elements of nationalism, and it may thus appear somewhat unfair and unrealistic to expect to find a completely objective attitude in Herder's work. Nevertheless this spirit of nationalism links him with his predecessors in France, England and Germany, and separates him from the mainstream of comparative literature in the twentieth century. The nationalistic approach to comparative literature reached its peak and then declined in the course of the nineteenth century; it neither began nor finished with Herder.

Unlike his predecessors, however, Herder was fully conscious of the nationalistic tendency in his comparative criticism and still saw nothing wrong in it, despite the fact that it conflicted with the theory of relativity, which he also supported. A similar conflict occurred in the writings of several earlier critics; we saw, for example, how Voltaire dismissed, in principle, all universal rules, but still used certain rules as a yardstick by which to measure the French theatre against the English theatre and rate the former above the latter. Yet he gave no indication that he was aware of the bias in his work. Herder, on the other hand, clearly stated in the final letter of the eighth collection of the *Humanitätsbriefe* that he regarded as perfectly legitimate a definite bias in any critic's work towards the literature of his own nation. He did not, however, make any attempt to reconcile nationalism with relativism: indeed, he apparently did not see that the problem existed.

The incongruity of Herder's nationalism and his relativism represents the opposition between the older and the more modern elements in his comparative criticism. The idea of relativity is a fundamental part of modern comparative literature. Certainly it is not a discovery of the twentieth century and many writers before Herder accepted the idea; but it was still possible for a critic of the seventeenth or eighteenth century to look at international literature from a fixed point of view. The works of Rapin, Rymer and Gottsched were acceptable to many of their countrymen, since the rules by which they judged foreign literature were generally taken for granted. Their type of criticism has scarcely been possible since the overthrow of neo-classicism in the eighteenth century. Such a doctrinaire attitude towards literature is today generally (although not exclusively) confined to totalitarian states.

Two of the most lively defences of relativism in recent times are to be found in the writings of Frederick Pottle and F. L. Lucas. In *The Idiom of Poetry* Pottle formulates succinctly the doctrine of critical relativism:

1 *Poetry always expresses the basis of feeling (or sensibility) of the age in which it was written.*

2 *Critics of the past were as well qualified to apply a subjective test to poetry as we are.*

3 *Poetry is whatever has been called poetry by respectable judges at any time and in any place.* ("Respectable" may be thought to beg the question. I mean to include in the term those critics who had the esteem of their own age, as well as those whom we admire.)

4 *The poetry of an age never goes wrong.* Culture may go wrong, civilization may go wrong, criticism may go wrong, but poetry, in the collective sense, cannot go wrong.[1]

It is almost impossible to trace the history of an idea such as that of relativity back to its first utterance. Lucas cites an example from the work of Herodotus[2] and we have seen how many of the critics discussed in this study, including some of the earliest, subscribed to the theory. Yet Herder expounded the idea more clearly and more completely than any previous critic. In the theoretical section at the end of the eighth col-

---

[1] Frederick A. Pottle, *The Idiom of Poetry* (Ithaca, N.Y., 1941), p. 21.
[2] F. L. Lucas, *Literature and Psychology* (London, 1951), p. 188.

lection he put forward most of the propositions which Pottle uses in his defence of relativism. In his survey of European literature in the latter part of the seventh and the first part of the eighth collection Herder adhered to the principle of relativity more faithfully than any of the earlier critics.

Perhaps it is appropriate and not altogether far-fetched to explain Herder's great reputation as a comparatist by the society and the period in which he lived. He arrived at a time when German interest in foreign literature was on the increase; writers such as Bodmer, Schlegel, Lessing and Meinhard had prepared the way for him. Gottsched and the neo-classical rules had already been cast aside and German literature was ready for a great new period. Herder's collection of folksongs and investigation of the manner in which the literature of other European countries reflected the genius of the various nations acted as a great stimulus. As Prof. Gillies has pointed out,[1] Friederich Schlegel owed much more to Herder than he was prepared to admit in his unfavourable review of the seventh and eighth collections of the *Humanitätsbriefe*.

Herder's work, and especially these collections of the *Humanitätsbriefe*, was an important prelude to the universality of the Romantic period. The fact that he did not bring any fundamentally new ideas or methods to the study of comparative literature does not significantly reduce his stature as a comparatist. He expressed ideas which were already current more forcefully than any previous critic and put them forward at the right historical moment. His tremendous enthusiasm and eagerness to understand the literature of many different nations exercised a profound influence on succeeding generations. Regardless of his originality he was extraordinarily successful in achieving his most important goals. He certainly contributed much to the great rise of German letters and caused men in many different countries to think in terms of world literature.

---

[1] A. Gillies, "Herder's preparation of Romantic theory," *Modern Language Review*, xxxix (1944), 252-261.

BIBLIOGRAPHY

Works relating to Herder

AUERBACH, ERICH. "Vico und Herder," *Deutsche Vierteljahrschrift für Literaturwissenschaft und Geistesgeschichte*, X (1932), 671-686.

BERLIN, SIR ISAIAH. "J. G. Herder," *Encounter*, XXV, 1 (July, 1965), 29-48. 2 (August, 1965), 42-51.

CLARK, ROBERT T. *Herder: his life and thought*. Berkeley: University of California Press, 1955.

CLARK, ROBERT T. "Herder's conception of 'Kraft'," *PMLA*. LVII, 3 (September, 1942), 737-752.

CLARK, ROBERT T. "Herder, Cesarotti and Vico," *Studies in Philology*, XLIV, 4 (October, 1947), 645-671.

CLOSS, AUGUST. "Wurzeln der Romantik bei Herder," *Modern Language Quarterly*, II (1941), 611-618.

DOBBEK, WILHELM. *J. G. Herders Humanitätsidee als Ausdruck seines Weltbildes und seiner Persönlichkeit*. Braunschweig: Georg Westermann Verlag, 1949.

ERGANG, ROBERT H. *Herder and the Foundations of German Nationalism* New York: Columbia University Press, 1931.

GILLIES, ALEXANDER. *Herder*. Oxford: Basil Blackwell, 1945.

GILLIES, ALEXANDER. "Herder and the Preparation of Goethe's Idea of Weltliteratur," *Publications of the English Goethe Society*, N. S. IX (1933), 46-67.

GILLIES, ALEXANDER. "Herder's Preparation of Romantic Theory," *Modern Language Review*, XXXIX (1944), 252-261.

HAGENBRING, PAUL. *Herder und die romantischen und nationalen Strömungen in der deutschen Literatur des 18. Jahrhunderts bis 1771*. Halle: Karras, 1911.

HAYM, RUDOLF. *Herder nach seinem Leben und seinen Werken dargestellt*. 2 vols., Berlin: R. Gaertner, 1877-1885.

HERDER, JOHANN GOTTFRIED VON. *Sämmtliche Werke*. ed. Bernhard Suphan. 33 vols., Berlin: Weidmannsche Buchhandlung, 1877-1913.

HERDER, JOHANN GOTTFRIED VON. *Werke*. ed. H. Meyer, H. Lambel and E. Kühnemann. 5 vols. Stuttgart: Union, 1889-1894 (= Deutsche National-Litteratur 74-77).

JORET, C. *Herder et la renaissance littéraire en Allemagne au XVIIIe siècle.* Paris: Hachette, 1875.

KOHLSCHMIDT, WERNER. *Herder-Studien: Untersuchungen zu Herders kritischem Stil und seinen literaturkritischen Grundeinsichten.* Berlin: Juncker und Dünnhaupt, 1929.

KOLLER, ARMIN H. *The Abbé Du Bos – His Advocacy of the Theory of Climate. A Precursor of Johann Gottfried Herder.* Champaign, Ill. Garrard Press, 1937.

KÜHNEMANN, EUGEN. *Herder.* 2nd ed. Munich: C. H. Beck, 1912.

REED, EUGENE E. "Herder, Primitivism and the Age of Poetry," *Modern Language Review,* LX (1965), 553-567.

RUNACHER, S. "Les diverses activités de Herder." *Études Germaniques,* XII (1957), 312-330.

SCHORK, LUISE. "Herders Bekanntschaft mit der englischen Literatur," *Beiträge zur Erforschung der Sprache und Kultur Englands und Nordamerikas,* Beiheft, 1928.

SCHÜTZE, MARTIN. "The Fundamental Ideas of Herder's Thought," *Modern Philology,* XVIII (1920-21), 65-78, 289-303; XIX (1921-22), 113-130, 361-382; XXI (1923), 29-48, 113-132.

STOLPE, HEINZ. *Die Auffassung des jungen Herder vom Mittelalter.* Weimar: Hermann Böhlaus Nachfolger, 1955.

ULRICH, GISELA. *Herders Beitrag zur Deutschkunde unter besonderer Berücksichtigung seiner literaturwissenschaftlichen Theorie.* Würzburg: K. Triltsch, 1943.

WEDEL, MAX. *Herder als Kritiker.* Berlin: E. Ebering, 1928.

WOLFF, HANS M. "Der junge Herder und die Entwicklungsidee Rousseaus," *PMLA,* LVII (1942), 753-819.

General works

ASCOLI, GEORGES. *La critique littéraire au XVIIe siècle.* Paris: Centre de Documentation Universitaire, 1937.

ATKINS, J. W. H. *English literary criticism: 17th and 18th centuries.* London: Methuen, 1951.

BALDENSPERGER, FERNAND. "Littérature comparée: le mot et la chose," *Revue de Littérature Comparée,* I (1921), 5-29.

BALDENSPERGER, FERNAND and FRIEDERICH, WERNER P. *Bibliography of Comparative Literature.* Chapel Hill: The University of North Carolina Press, 1950.

BARON, HANS. "The Querelle des anciens et des modernes as a problem for renaissance scholarship," *Journal of the History of Ideas,* XX (1959), 3-22.

BENDER, HELMUT and MELZER, ULRICH. "Zur Geschichte des Begriffes 'Weltliteratur'," *Saeculum,* IX (1953), 113-123.

BETZ, LOUIS. "Litteraturvergleichung," *Das litterarische Echo,* X (1901), 657-665.

BOSKER, A. *Literary Criticism in the Age of Johnson.* 2nd ed., rev. Groningen: J. B. Wolters, 1953.

BOURGOIN, AUGUSTE. *Les maîtres de la critique au XVIIe siècle.* Paris: Garnier, 1889.

BRAITMAIER, FRIEDRICH. *Geschichte der poetischen Theorie und Kritik.* Frauenfeld: J. Huber, 1889.

148

BRUNETIÈRE, FERDINAND. *L'évolution des genres dans l'histoire de la littérature.* Paris: Hachette, 1890.

BUCK, AUGUST. "Aus der Vorgeschichte der 'Querelle des Anciens et des Modernes' in Mittelalter und Renaissance," *Bibliothèque d'Humanisme et de Renaissance,* XX (1958), 527-541.

CHANDLER, FRANK W. "The Comparative Study of Literature," *Yearbook of Comparative and General Literature,* XV (1966), 50-62.

CORSTIUS, JAN BRANDT. *Introduction to the Comparative Study of Literature.* New York: Random House, 1968.

CORSTIUS, JAN BRANDT. "The impact of cosmopolitanism and nationalism on comparative literature from the beginning to 1880," *Proceedings of the IVth Congress of the International Comparative Literature Association,* The Hague: Mouton & Co., 1966, 380-389.

ERNST, FRITZ. *Die Schweiz als geistige Mittlerin von Muralt bis Jacob Burckhardt.* Zürich: Verlag der neuen Schweizer Rundschau, 1932.

ÉTIEMBLE, RENÉ. *Comparaison n'est pas raison; la crise de la littérature comparée.* Paris: Gallimard, 1963.

ÉTIEMBLE, RENÉ. "Faut-il réviser la notion de Weltliteratur?" *Proceedings of the IVth Congress of the International Comparative Literature Association,* The Hague: Mouton & Co., 1966, 5-16.

FLEISCHMANN, WOLFGANG B. "Das Arbeitsgebiet der Vergleichenden Literaturwissenschaft," *Arcadia,* I (1966), 221-230.

GILLOT, HUBERT. *La Querelle des Anciens et des Modernes en France.* Nancy: A. Crépin-Leblond, 1914.

GUÉRARD, ALBERT LÉON. *Preface to World Literature.* New York: H. Holt, 1940.

GUÉRARD, ALBERT LÉON. "Comparative Literature?," *Yearbook of Comparative and General Literature VII* (1958), 1-6.

GUYARD, MARIUS-FRANÇOIS. *La littérature comparée.* Paris: Presses Universitaires de France, 1951.

JANTZ, HAROLD. "The Fathers of Comparative Literature," *Books Abroad,* X (1936), 401-403.

KRAUSS, WERNER. *Studien zur deutschen und französischen Aufklärung.* Berlin: Rütten und Loening, 1963.

KRAUSS, WERNER and KORTUM, HANS. *Antike und Moderne in der Literaturdiskussion des 18. Jahrhunderts.* Berlin: Akademie Verlag, 1966.

LEMPICKI, SIGMUND VON. *Geschichte der deutschen Literaturwissenschaft bis zum Ende des 18. Jahrhunderts.* Göttingen: Vandenhoeck and Ruprecht, 1920.

LUCAS, F. L. *Literature and Psychology.* London: Cassell, 1951.

MILLER, GEORGE M. *The historical point of view in English literary criticism from 1570-1770.* Heidelberg: C. Winter, 1913.

MOREAU, PIERRE. *La Critique littéraire en France.* Paris: Armand Colin, 1960.

PERRAULT, CHARLES. *Parallèle des Anciens et des Modernes en ce qui regarde les Arts et les Sciences.* München: Eidos Verlag, 1964.

PETERSEN, JULIUS. "Nationale oder vergleichende Literaturgeschichte?," *Deutsche Vierteljahrschrift für Literaturwissenschaft und Geistesgeschichte,* VI (1928), 36-61.

149

PICHOIS, CLAUDE et ROUSSEAU, ANDRÉ-M. *La Littérature Comparée*. Paris: Armand Colin, 1967.

POSNETT, H. M. *Comparative Literature*. New York: Appleton, 1886.

POTTLE, FREDERICK A. *The Idiom of Poetry*. Ithaca, N.Y.: Cornell University Press, 1941.

PRICE, LAWRENCE M. *English Literature in Germany*. Berkeley: University of California Press, 1953.

REMAK, HENRY H. H. "Comparative Literature at the Crossroads: Diagnosis, Therapy and Prognosis," *Yearbook of Comparative and General Literature*, IX (1960), 1-28.

REMAK, HENRY H. H. "Comparative Literature, Its Definition and Function," In Newton P. Stallknecht and Horst Frenz, eds. *Comparative Literature: Method and Perspective*. Carbondale: Southern Illinois University Press, 1961.

ROBERTSON, JOHN G. *Studies in the Genesis of Romantic Theory in the Eighteenth Century*. Cambridge: The University Press, 1923.

RÜDIGER, HORST. "Nationalliteraturen und europäische Literatur," *Schweizer Monatshefte*, XLII (1962), 195-211.

SAINTSBURY, GEORGE. *A History of Criticism and Literary Taste in Europe*. 3 vols. Edinburgh: Blackwood, 1900-1904.

SCHULTZ, FRANZ. "Die Entwicklung der Literaturwissenschaft von Herder bis Wilhelm Scherer." In Emil Ermatinger, ed. *Philosophie der Literaturwissenschaft*. Berlin: Juncker und Dünnhaupt, 1930.

SMITH, DAVID NICHOL. *Eighteenth Century Essays on Shakespeare*. New York: Russell and Russell, 1962.

STRICH, FRITZ. "Weltliteratur und vergleichende Literaturgeschichte." In Emil Ermatinger, ed. *Philosophie der Literaturwissenschaft*. Berlin: Juncker und Dünnhaupt, 1930.

TEXTE, JOSEPH. *Études de littérature européene*. Paris: A. Colin, 1898.

VAN TIEGHEM, PAUL. *La littérature comparée*. Paris: A. Colin, 1931.

WAIS, KURT. "Le cosmopolitisme littéraire à travers les ages." *Proceedings of the IVth Congress of the International Comparative Literature Association*, The Hague: Mouton & Co., 1966, 17-29.

WELLEK, RENÉ. *A History of Modern Criticism: 1750-1950*. 4 vols., New Haven: Yale University Press, 1955-1965.

WELLEK, RENÉ. *The Rise of English Literary History*. Chapel Hill: University of North Carolina Press, 1941.

WELLEK, RENÉ. "The Crisis of Comparative Literature," *Proceedings of the Second Congress of the International Comparative Literature Association*, I (1959), 149-159.

WELLEK, RENÉ. "Begriff und Idee der Vergleichenden Literaturwissenschaft," *Arcadia*, II (1967), 229-247.

WELLEK, RENÉ and WARREN, AUSTIN. *Theory of Literature*. 3rd ed., New York: Harcourt Brace, 1956.

Works relating to individual authors

ADDISON, JOSEPH. *Works.* ed. Richard Hurd, 6 vols. London: G. Bell, 1888-1892.

BEATTIE, JAMES. *Dissertations Moral and Critical.* 2 vols. Dublin, 1783.

BERTRAM, PHILLIP ERNST. *Entwurf einer Geschichte der Gelahrheit.* Halle, 1764.

BIEDERMANN, WOLDEMAR FREIHERR VON. ed. *Goethes Gespräche.* 10 vols. Leipzig: Biedermann, 1889-1896.

BLACKWELL, THOMAS. *An Enquiry into the Life and Writings of Homer.* London, 1735.

BLAIR, HUGH. *Lectures on Rhetoric and Belles Lettres.* ed. Harold F. Harding, 2 vols. Carbondale: Southern Illinois University Press, 1965.

BODMER, J. J. *Critische Betrachtungen über die poetischen Gemählde der Dichter.* Zürich, 1741.

BODMER, J. J. and BREITINGER, J. J. *Von dem Einfluss und Gebrauche der Einbildungs-Krafft zur Ausbesserung des Geschmackes.* Frankfurt and Leipzig, 1727.

BROWN, JOHN. *A Dissertation on the Rise, Union, and Power, the Progressions, Separations, and Corruptions, of Poetry and Music.* London, 1763.

DEIMIER, PIERRE DE. *L'Académie de l'Art poétique.* Paris, 1610.

DU BELLAY, JOACHIM. *La deffence et illustration de la langue françoyse.* ed. Henri Chamard, Paris: M. Didier, 1948.

DUBOS, JEAN BAPTISTE. *Réflexions critiques sur la poésie et sur la peinture.* 3 vols. Paris, 1733.

DURHAM, WILLARD H. ed. *Critical Essays of the Eighteenth Century, 1700-1725.* New Haven: Yale University Press, 1915.

ELLEDGE, SCOTT. ed. *Eighteenth Century Critical Essays.* 2 vols. Ithaca, N.Y.: Cornell University Press, 1961.

FEIND, BARTHOLD. *Deutsche Gedichte.* Stade, 1708.

FIELDING, HENRY. *Works.* ed. Leslie Stephen, 10 vols. London: Smith, Elder and Co., 1882.

GERSTENBERG, HEINRICH WILHELM VON. *Briefe über Merkwürdigkeiten der Litteratur.* ed. Alexander von Weilen, Stuttgart: G. J. Göschen, 1890.

GOLDSMITH, OLIVER. *Works.* ed. Peter Cunningham, 4 vols. London: J. Murray, 1854.

GOSSE, SIR EDMUND W. *Two Pioneers of Romanticism: Joseph and Thomas Warton.* London: Oxford University Press, 1915.

GOTTSCHED, JOHANN CHRISTOPH. *Versuch einer critischen Dichtkunst.* Reprint of 4th ed. Leipzig, 1751. Darmstadt: Wissenschaftliche Gesellschaft, 1962.

GUNDOLF, FRIEDRICH. *Shakespeare und der deutsche Geist.* Berlin: G. Bondi, 1922.

HAVENS, RAYMOND D. "Thomas Warton and the Eighteenth Century Dilemma," *Studies in Philology*, XXV (1928), 36-50.

HAYLEY, WILLIAM. *An Essay on Epic Poetry.* London: Dodsley, 1782.

HEWETT-THAYER, HARVEY W. *Laurence Sterne in Germany: a contribution to the study of the literary relations of England and Germany in the eighteenth century.* New York: Columbia University Press, 1905.

HILL, GEORGE B. N. ed. *Boswell's Life of Johnson.* Rev. and enl. ed. by L. F. Powell. 6 vols. Oxford: The Clarendon Press, 1934-1950.

HOFMANNSWALDAU, CHRISTIAN HOFMANN VON. *Deutsche Übersetzungen und Gedichte.* Breslau, 1710.

151

HURD, RICHARD. *Letters on Chivalry and Romance.* ed. Edith J. Morley, London: H. Frowde, 1911.

JOHNSON, SAMUEL. *Works.* ed. Sir John Hawkins, 11 vols. London: 1787.

KIND, JOHN LOUIS. *Edward Young in Germany.* New York: Columbia University Press, 1906.

KRAUSS, WERNER. *Cartaud de la Villate.* 2 vols. Berlin: Akademie Verlag, 1960.

LESSING, GOTTHOLD EPHRAIM. *Sämtliche Schriften.* ed. Karl Lachmann, 3rd rev. ed. F. Muncker, 23 vols. Stuttgart and Leipzig: J. G. Göschen, 1886-1924.

LOUNSBURY, THOMAS R. *The Text of Shakespeare.* New York: C. Scribner's Sons, 1906.

MEISTER, J. G. *Unvorgreifliche Gedancken von Teutschen Epigrammatibus.* Leipzig, 1726.

MENDELSSOHN, MOSES. *Gesammelte Schriften.* ed. G. B. Mendelssohn. 7 vols. Leipzig: F. U. Brockhaus, 1843-1845.

MERIAN-GENAST, ERNST. "Voltaire und die Entwicklung der Idee der Weltliteratur," *Romanische Forschungen,* XL (1927), 1-226.

MEYER, RICHARD M. ed. *Goethe und seine Freunde im Briefwechsel.* 3 vols. Berlin: G. Bondi, 1909-1911.

MONCHOUX, ANDRÉ. "Sébastien Mercier." *Proceedings of the IVth Congress of the International Comparative Literature Association,* The Hague: Mounton & Co., 1966, 30-42.

MONTESQUIEU, CHARLES LOUIS DE SECONDAT, Baron de La Brède et de. *Œuvres complètes.* ed. Roger Caillois. 2 vols. Paris: Gallimard, 1949-1951.

MORHOF, DANIEL GEORG. *Unterricht von der Teutschen Sprache und Poesie.* Kiel, 1682.

MURALT, BÉAT LOUIS DE. *Lettres sur les Anglois et les François et sur les voiages.* ed. Charles Gould. Paris: H. Champion, 1933.

NÄF, WERNER. *Vadian und seine Stadt St. Gallen.* 2 vols. St. Gallen: Fehr'sche Buchhandlung, 1944-57.

NICOLAI, CHRISTOPH FRIEDRICH. *Briefe über den itzigen Zustand der schönen Wissenschaften in Deutschland.* ed. G. Ellinger, Berlin: Paetal, 1894.

OPITZ, MARTIN. *Buch von der deutschen Poeterey.* ed. Richard Alewyn, Tübingen: M. Niemeyer, 1963.

PASQUIER, ÉTIENNE. *Œuvres choisies.* ed. Léon Feugère. 2 vols. Paris: Firmin Didot Frères, 1849.

RAPIN, RENÉ. *Œuvres.* 3 vols. The Hague: P. Grosse, 1725.

REHDER, HELMUT. *Johann Nicolaus Meinhard und seine Übersetzungen.* Urbana: University of Illinois Press, 1953.

RINAKER, CLARISSA. *Thomas Warton; a biographical and critical study.* Urbana: University of Illinois Press, 1916. Reviewed by Odell Shepard, *JEGP,* XVI (1917), 153-163.

SAINT-ÉVREMOND, CHARLES DE MARGUETEL DE SAINT DENIS, Seigneur de. *Œuvres mêlées.* ed. Charles Giraud. 3 vols. Paris: J. L. Techener, 1865.

SCHLEGEL, FRIEDRICH VON. *Prosaische Jugendschriften.* ed. J. Minor. Vienna: Carl Konegen, 1882.

SCHLEGEL, JOHANN ELIAS. *Ausgewählte Werke.* ed. W. Schubert. Weimar: Arion Verlag, 1963.

SOMMERFELD, MARTIN. *Friedrich Nicolai und der Sturm und Drang; ein Beitrag zur Geschichte der deutschen Aufklärung.* Halle: Max Niemeyer, 1921.

SPINGARN, JOEL ELIAS. ed. *Critical Essays of the Seventeenth Century.* 3 vols. Oxford: The Clarendon Press, 1908.

STERNE, LAURENCE. *The Life and Opinions of Tristram Shandy, Gentleman.* ed. James A. Work. New York: The Odyssey Press, 1940.

STOLLE, GOTTLIEB. *Anleitung zur Historie der Gelahrtheit.* Jena, 1727.

STRICH, FRITZ. *Goethe und die Weltliteratur.* Bern: Francke Verlag, 1957.

TEXTE, JOSEPH. *Jean-Jacques Rousseau and the Cosmopolitan Spirit in Literature.* Tr. J. W. Matthews. London: Duckworth and Co., 1899.

URFÉ, HONORÉ D'. *La Sylvanire; ou, La Morte-vive.* Paris: R. Fouet, 1627.

VILLATE, N. CARTAUD DE LA. *Essai historique et philosophique sur le goût.* Amsterdam, 1735.

VIOLLET-LE-DUC, EMMANUEL. ed. *Ancien théâtre françois.* 10 vols. Paris: P. Jannet, 1854-1857.

VOLTAIRE, FRANÇOIS MARIE AROUET DE. *Œuvres complètes.* ed. Louis Moland. 52 vols. Paris: Garnier Frères, 1877-1885.

WARTON, JOSEPH. *An Essay on the Genius and Writings of Pope.* 5th ed. 2 vols. London: W. J. and J. Richardson, 1806.

WARTON, THOMAS. *Observations on the Fairy Queen of Spenser.* 2nd ed. 2 vols. London: R. and J. Dodsley, 1762.

WARTON, THOMAS. *The History of English Poetry, from the Close of the Eleventh to the Commencement of the Eighteenth Century.* 4 vols. London: J. Dodsley et. al., 1775-1781.

WEHRLI, MAX. *Johann Jakob Bodmer und die Geschichte der Literatur.* Frauenfeld and Leipzig: Huber, 1936.

WHITE, FLORENCE DONNELL. *Voltaire's Essay on Epic Poetry; a Study and an Edition.* Albany, N.Y.: The Brandow Printing Co., 1915.

YOUNG, EDWARD. *Conjectures on Original Composition.* ed. Edith J. Morley. Manchester: The University Press, 1918.

REPRINTS FROM OUR COMPARATIVE LITERATURE STUDIES

Through the University of North Carolina Press
Chapel Hill, North Carolina 27514

2 Werner P. Friederich. DANTE'S FAME ABROAD, 1350-1850. The Influence of Dante Alighieri on the Poets and Scholars of Spain, France, England, Germany, Switzerland and the United States. Rome, 1950; Third Printing, 1966. Pp. 584. Paper, $10.00.

10 Charles E. Passage. DOSTOEVSKI THE ADAPTER. A Study in Dostoevski's Use of the Tales of Hoffmann. 1954. Reprinted, 1963. Pp. x, 205. Paper, $3.50. Cloth, $4.50

11 Werner P. Friederich and David H. Malone. OUTLINE OF COMPARATIVE LITERATURE. From Dante Alighieri to Eugene O'Neill. 1954. Fourth Printing, 1967. Pp. 460. Paper, $6.50.

Through Russell and Russell, Inc. Publishers,
122 East 42 Street, New York, New York 10017

1 Fernand Baldensperger and Werner P. Friederich. BIBLIOGRAPHY OF COMPARATIVE LITERATURE. 1950. Pp. 729. Cloth, $15.00.

6 7, 9, 14, 16, 18, 21, 25, and 27. W. P. Friederich and H. Frenz (eds): YEARBOOKS OF COMPARATIVE AND GENERAL LITERATURE. Vols. 1 (1952) to IX (1960). Cloth, $7.50 per volume.

Through Johnson Reprint Corporation
111 Fifth Avenue, New York, New York 10003

3 R. C. Simonini, Jr. ITALIAN SCHOLARSHIP IN RENAISSANCE ENGLAND. Cloth, $12.50.

4 GOETHE'S SORROWS OF YOUNG WERTER, TRANSLATED BY GEORGE TICKNOR. Edited with Introduction and Critical Analysis by Frank G. Ryder. Cloth, $8.00.

5 Helmut A. Hatzfeld. A CRITICAL BIBLIOGRAPHY OF THE NEW STYLISTICS APPLIED TO THE ROMANCE LITERATURES, 1900-1952. Cloth, $12.00.

13 Horst Frenz and G. L. Anderson, eds. INDIANA UNIVERSITY CONFERENCE ON ORIENTAL-WESTERN LITERARY RELATIONS. Cloth, $15.00.

15 Dorothy B. Schlegel. SHAFTESBURY AND THE FRENCH DEISTS. Cloth, $12.50.

19 P. A. Shelley, A. O. Lewis Jr. and W. W. Betts Jr., eds. ANGLO-GERMAN AND AMERICAN-GERMAN CROSSCURRENTS, Volume One. Cloth, $15.00.

22 Harvey W. Hewett-Thayer. AMERICAN LITERATURE AS VIEWED IN GERMANY, 1818-1861. Cloth, $8.50.

UNIVERSITY OF NORTH CAROLINA
STUDIES IN COMPARATIVE LITERATURE

42 W. LaMarr Kopp. GERMAN LITERATURE IN THE UNITED STATES, 1945-1960. Volume III of Anglo-German and German-American Cross-currents, Philip A. Shelley and Arthur O. Lewis, Editors. 1967. Pp. xx, 230. Cloth, $7.50.

43 James I. Wimsatt. CHAUCER AND THE FRENCH LOVE POETS: THE LITERARY BACKGROUND OF THE BOOK OF THE DUCHESS. 1968. Pp. ix, 186. Cloth, $6.50.

44 Yvonne Rodax. THE REAL AND THE IDEAL IN THE NOVELLA OF ITALY, FRANCE AND ENGLAND. Four Centuries of Change in the Boccaccian Tale. 1968. Pp. ix, 138. Cloth, $5.50.

45 Herbert W. Reichert and Karl Schlechta. INTERNATIONAL NIETZSCHE BIBLIOGRAPHY. Revised and Expanded. 1968. Pp. xvii, 162. Cloth, $8.00.

46 Clarence Gohdes, Ed. RUSSIAN STUDIES OF AMERICAN LITERATURE; A BIBLIOGRAPHY. Compiled by Valentina A. Libman. Translated by Robert V. Allen. 1969. Pp. xiv, 217. Cloth, $8.00.

47 Garold N. Davis. GERMAN THOUGHT AND CULTURE IN ENGLAND, 1700-1770. A Preliminary Survey, Including a Chronological Bibliography of German Literature in English Translation. 1969. Pp. 140. Cloth, $5.50.

48 Robert S. Mayo. HERDER AND THE BEGINNINGS OF COMPARATIVE LITERATURE. 1969. Pp. 000. Cloth, $0.00.